TWENTIETH CENTURY INTERPRETATIONS
OF

THE EVE
OF ST. AGNES

A Collection of Critical Essays

Edited by
ALLAN DANZIG

Prentice-Hall, Inc.  Englewood Cliffs, N. J.
A SPECTRUM BOOK

Copyright © 1971 by Prentice-Hall, Inc., Englewood Cliffs, New Jersey. A
SPECTRUM BOOK. All rights reserved. No part of this book may be reproduced in any form or by any means without permission in writing from the
publisher. C–13-292219-3; P–13-292201-0. *Library of Congress Catalog Card Number: 70–140268.* Printed in the United States of America.

Current printing (last number):
10 9 8 7 6 5 4 3 2 1

PRENTICE-HALL INTERNATIONAL, INC. (*London*)
PRENTICE-HALL OF AUSTRALIA, PTY. LTD. (*Sydney*)
PRENTICE-HALL OF CANADA, LTD. (*Toronto*)
PRENTICE-HALL OF INDIA PRIVATE LIMITED (*New Delhi*)
PRENTICE-HALL OF JAPAN, INC. (*Tokyo*)

Contents

iii

TWENTIETH CENTURY INTERPRETATIONS
OF
THE EVE OF ST. AGNES

Introduction

by Allan Danzig

John Keats had the shortest life of any major English poet. Despite this bare fact, and despite the passage of over 150 years since his death, he still seems one of the most alive. Through his poetry we participate minutely in the development of his imagination and his art. In his letters, unmatched in English for their combination of wholly personal revelation and general public interest, we can watch a personality forging itself, week by week and almost day by day. We consider it a measure of Shakespeare's strength that the art conceals the man. In the case of other, "finished" poets like Tennyson, whose long productive lives gave them time to work themselves fully into art, their poetry becomes a sufficient monument behind which we have little need to look. But Keats, who wrote all his best poetry in little more than a year after a short if painfully intense apprenticeship, remains a man distinct and knowable. Indeed, the problem often seems which Keats to know, for like any intimate—indeed, like ourselves—he presents a number of changing faces we can only imperfectly bring into focus.

Doubtless most widely known is the ethereal Keats, dreamy poet of the legend. In many ways this is a pity, for an unworldly delicacy is not what the twentieth century admires in its poets. Yet this view does not appear to do Keats much harm today, and unquestionably helped establish his reputation among nineteenth century readers. In "Adonais," his elegy on Keats's death, Shelley introduced readers to a hothouse flower, a poet so fragile his life was snuffed out by a hostile review. Shelley's images of melting star and wind-bruised blossom come from Keats's own poetry, and are by now probably indissolubly part of his biography. They remind us he was the tepid and rather gushy disciple of Leigh Hunt, and a player of tedious poetic games—sessions of extemporaneous effusions and *bouts rimés;*

the self-conscious exchange of floral chaplets and laurel wreaths. This is the Keats of the blasted life, the romantic death. It is indeed possible to support this sentimental view of the poet, but it is well to remember that its most tangible evidence is the wan face of the death mask.

For another Keats breaks through the remote if undeniable beauty of the cold plaster: the sturdy ostler's son with a body like a barrel. As a schoolboy Keats was far more attracted by the rough and tumble of games at recess than by his books. Students and masters expected he would go to sea or even become a prize-fighter though he was barely over five feet tall. This is our first view of the genial young man who enjoyed the grotesque and the bawdy, and who would tramp across London to meet friends and flirt with their sisters. We see him again on his tour into Scotland, walking with a pack on his pack thirty miles a day, climbing mountains, soaked to the skin by rains that turned the path into a river. His growing love of Fanny Brawne, it is increasingly clear, was no yearning for a disembodied spirit. Determined to be an honorable lover, he was tormented by love—or was it lust? He worried, unresolved. This Keats of strenuous physical life and appetites shades into the experimenter of the senses, proposing pleasurable shocks to disorder and extend his perceptions. His friend Benjamin Haydon complained that Keats "once covered his tongue and throat as far as he could reach with Cayenne pepper in order to appreciate the 'delicious coldness of claret in all its glory'—his own expression." [1] But despite Haydon's disapproval, Keats drank and wenched when he could, as on his visit to Oxford.

And here another Keats emerges. For his host at Oxford, Benjamin Bailey, was a student of theology (he eventually became a fairly colorless mid-Victorian clergyman, his student excesses decently forgotten). With him Keats discussed questions of philosophy

---

[1] Benjamin Haydon, *Autobiography*, ed. Alexander Penrose (M. Balch & Co., 1929), p. 259. There is some question as to whether Keats actually carried out this program or merely teased Haydon with the idea. It seems a rather harmless trick, in any case. Most noteworthy about it is the echo, conscious or not, of the Russian practice of chewing black pepper before drinking vodka iced to the consistency of syrup. Perhaps Keats read of the habit somewhere, or learned of it from his guardian John Nowland Sandell, a "Russia merchant" or leather dealer.

and poetic theory. In his letters to Bailey and others Keats shows himself a craftsman passionately concerned with his art. If in the realm of ideas he seems more enthusiastic than original, and rarely very deep or systematic, he is always a graceful thinker. His philosophy does not make a coherent whole—we could scarcely ask this of a man whose thinking life ended, apparently, at the age of twenty-four—but his critique of "consequitive reasoning," his distinction between the reflective and the spontaneous, and between the objective and the subjective personality, remain lively and helpful today. His insights have changed the way we think about poetry, and this means, finally, the way we view the world. His critical perceptions of other poets, and his acute understanding of what he was trying to achieve in his own work, are evaluations more precise than what we would expect from either Keats the dreamer or the man of the body.

Added to these are various minor yet sharply defined roles, each with its glimpse of an essential Keats: the warm-hearted brother (however special and distinct his relationships with George, Tom, and Frances, they are uniformly tender); the successful medical student; the lover of jokes and puns; the young man shy and proud, troubled by his lack of stature and jealous of his status as a gentleman. Finally there is Keats hero of a tragedy of waste: his father's meaningless death, his mother's wasted love, the waste of his inheritance through his guardians' negligence; the blind alleys explored by his late-awakening genius; the death of his brother Tom presaging his own two years later, and the painful separations from George and Frances; his vexatious love, capable of no fruitful conclusion; and the final wasting into death seemingly convinced that he had failed to produce poetry that would live.

These varied and at times contradictory personalities find their focus in the poetry, if at all. The thinker, the lover, the tragic hero, speak to us in the "Ode to a Nightingale"; "Endymion" shows the poet dreaming and yet robust, and "Isabella" how an appreciation of the grotesque need not drive out a taste for the sentimental. But "The Eve of St. Agnes" perhaps of all of Keats's poems presents the widest range of his aspects in their sharpest delineation. The dreamer contributes the unworldly delicacy of romance; immediate physical detail and sexual love come from the spokesman of the body. The sensualist charges the poem with its gorgeous colors and tastes. The thinker creates the myth of a waking world transformed by the reality of the dream. And the lover, struggling with tragedy, works out the conclusion of love triumphant in a hateful world. Balancing the widest, most inclusive—or most contrary—demands he made upon himself, and upon his world, "The Eve of St. Agnes" is Keats's most nearly all-embracing poem, and possibly his most successful.

In other poems, notably certain of the Odes, Keats may have examined specific insights more searchingly. For the ode is a lyric form, empowering the author to speak in his own voice (or one virtually indistinguishable from his), while following the turns and by-ways of his emotion to its harmonious resolution. The ode is, as well, traditionally free in its structure and elevated in tone; of all lyric forms it thus lends itself most easily to intellectual questioning, pursuit of an idea to a logically satisfying conclusion. It is therefore uniquely suited to investigations into the shifting emotional nimbus surrounding the progressive unfolding of an idea, and particularization of the emerging emotion into what amounts to a personally valid intellectual certainty. It was to this use that Keats triumphantly put the ode in the spring of his grand year of poetry, 1819. But in the first months of that year Keats, working in a narrative mode, created in "The Eve of St. Agnes" an entire world, one entirely satisfying in dramatic terms.

Nearly all the authors of the essays in this collection make it clear that they agree with this evaluation. Each of them emphasizes some aspect of Keats's almost Blakean use of contraries, pointing out that dramatic oppositions establish the universe of the poem. All is cold and darkness at the opening, in contrast to the soft light and later the warmth of Madeline's bedchamber. The hate of the "outside" world heightens the love "within," at the heart of the castle and of the poem. Porphyro and Madeline, a young couple who find love in each other, balance the beadsman and Angela, a loveless pair who seem not even to know of each other's existence. And lest his contraries degenerate into a schema of merely intellectual absolutes, simple and lifeless, Keats complicates their polarities. "Love" is opposed not simply by "hate" but by three carefully distinguished kinds of lovelessness: the sensual fury of the revelers, the beadsman's denial of sensuality, and—her equivocal position serving as a bridge between those who love and those who cannot—Angela's conventional sentimentality. Thus Keats suggests a range of characterization. Playing our expectations of stock characters against emerging relationships, he makes the poem lifelike with the semblance of sophisticated gradations. The same process is at work among the settings and images of the poem. The contrary of the beadsman's dark chapel is not, as it first appears, the bright ballroom; each opposes in a significant way the moonlit bedchamber. Here Madeline preparing for bed reminds us of the carved angels of the ballroom; Porphyro kneeling in the moonlight may be taken for a funerary figure like those in the chapel. Images and values are thus constantly reviewed and renewed. Even love, the great positive value of the poem, is not presented in simple unitary terms. We see it first, imperfectly understood, in the romantic longings of Porphyro, in the superstitious ritual of Madeline; it slowly grows more realistic, as Keats refracts it through all of Porphyro's senses and in Madeline's dream, to its climax. Finally we see it completely alive, strong enough to brave the storm into which the lovers disappear. Shifting dramatic contrast makes "The Eve of St. Agnes" a poem of human process in a fully realized world.

It is a measure of Keats's success that "The Eve of St. Agnes" is at once so rich and so unequivocal. For among the many essays on the poem it is difficult to find any one that significantly contradicts another. There is a unanimity of critical opinion, concerning not only the worth of the poem but also what it says and the way it says it, that is unusual in the case of so complex a work. Even critics who start from diametrically opposed positions reveal broad areas of fundamental agreement. Thus Earl Wasserman holds that the poem was written by Keats the thinker, and makes of him a highly organized philosopher with an almost religious view. In Wasserman's reading, earthly love draws significance from its relation to a world of "finer tone" and higher meaning; Porphyro and Madeline become almost figures of allegory. Jack Stillinger, with emphatic earthiness, relentlessly portrays them as creatures of flesh and blood. Porphyro is a seducer, almost a rapist, and Madeline's silly romanticizing is finally dissolved by her recognition of a sexual predicament that may engulf her. Stillinger, insisting on the poet's skepticism toward any other-worldly claims, is clearly reading a poem written by Keats of the body. Yet even here, with lines of disagreement so clearly drawn, Wasserman centers the poem in its human relevance, while Stillinger draws back from what he cheerfully acknowledges to be sensationalism to admit the existence of love. Furthermore, the essay by Clifford Adelman advances a view which in effect accommodates both Wasserman's and Stillinger's. And this is as close to a Great Debate as we will find in twentieth century interpretations of "The Eve of St. Agnes." To be sure, Herbert Wright's essay, "Has Keats's 'Eve of St. Agnes' a Tragic Ending?," attempts to raise a more polemic issue, ingeniously presenting evidence to support an unusual point of view. But Wright's argument seems to be only an extreme statement of an idea other commentators quietly accept—that the lovers' future life "o'er the southern moors" is no simple Happily Ever After.

For the most part, critics have avoided basic reinterpretations. Nor have they fallen into the trivial skirmishing that often breaks out in the far provinces of a great poem; there has been, for example, no tiresome debate of a legitimate if minor question, whether the beadsman has literally died on the morning after the lovers' escape, or if his continued life is itself a sufficient kind of death. Interpreters have been content with slight changes of emphasis, usefully extending and enriching each others' readings. Walter Jackson Bate's essay is a master's summation, discussing the poem's genesis—its biographical background and Keats's psychological state when he wrote it—and analyzing its poetic techniques and effects. Bate swiftly and deftly reviews the entire poem, and examines several successive revisions and their meanings. One can hardly think there is much more to say, after this investigation. Yet Robert Gittings, going over much the same ground as Bate, deepens the relevance of the biographical material and significantly extends consideration of the poem's sources. He revises Bate's picture without denying its validity. Even Bernard Blackstone, who more than the others seems to go his own way—offering in many ways the most unusual interpretation presented here and diverging on several points, both small and large (rather than dismissing the beadsman's prayers as useless, he finds in them another valid aspect of love; he measures "The Eve of St. Agnes" against "Endymion," which he feels to be Keats's most significant work; he regards enchantment not as a possible evil or even fallacious perception, but as a positive good)—follows a parallel track rather than striking off at a wholly new angle.

With the possible exception of Byron, Keats is the only Romantic poet whose reputation has steadily increased in the twentieth century. This is in part due to our interest in the poet's biography, in part to the continuing significance of intellectual and critical problems raised by his poems. But primarily a poet remains alive because he can create in his readers a sense of participating in a many-layered, heightened reality, of extending their lives and "proving on the pulses" an intellectual, and finally a moral, perception. It is always the mark of a great poem that its reading persuades us that we have lived through an experience. It is for this special pleasure, the following essays agree, that readers continue to turn to "The Eve of St. Agnes."

Has Keats's "Eve of St. Agnes"
a Tragic Ending?

by Herbert G. Wright

In *The Eve of St. Agnes* it is the richness of the sensations, the
magic of the placenames and the haunting verbal music that most
commonly attract attention. These qualities are displayed in their
most exquisite form in the vision scene which quite naturally remains uppermost in the mind. But we ought not to forget that
Keats is writing a narrative poem and that the fate of the lovers
is the climax of the story that he has to tell. This point is therefore
all-important. Yet we are left in doubt. All that Keats says directly is:

> And they are gone: aye, ages long ago
> These lovers fled away into the storm.

Perhaps most readers, with the instinctive desire for a happy ending, are apt to assume that after the escape of Madeline and Porphyro all is well, and that they succeed in reaching the shelter of
the castle "o'er the southern moors." Nevertheless, it may be wondered whether Keats did not intend to suggest a very different
conclusion and whether throughout the poem he did not antici-
pate that the great adventure of the lovers would culminate in
disaster. In this connexion the part played by the elements deserves
consideration. At the beginning Keats employs all his resources to
convey the intensity of the cold, inside and outside the chapel.
Sometimes it is explained that his purpose was to draw a contrast

with the warmth of the castle. But in point of fact, this feeling of warmth is confined within narrow limits. We are aware of it only in the vision scene, and even here it is associated only with Madeline—the "warm gules" from the window reflected on her breast, her "warmed jewels" and the "poppied warmth" of her sleep. Certainly there is in this passage a deliberate contrast between the vital warmth of the heroine and the cold about her. However, it should be read in relation to the poem as a whole, and it may be surmised that Keats's general design aimed at something more than this artistic effect. The magnificence of the vision scene ought not to blind us to the dominant impression of bitter cold. Keats devotes the two opening stanzas of a not very lengthy poem to the creation of this atmosphere, and, as the story unfolds, allows it to lose none of its potency. Again and again he speaks of the cold in the castle on this night which has followed a wintry day. The room to which Angela guides Porphyro, the bedchamber, and even the bed of Madeline are described as chilly, and the waiting Porphyro is "pallid, chill, and drear."

Once the storm breaks, the cold seems to become still more numbing. The wintry moon which had shone through the room grows pallid, and before long even this dimness fades away as the moon sets. The extinction of its light coincides with and marks the end of the happiness of the lovers. All is now dark, and the sleet patters against the panes. The wind increases in violence, and "the iced gusts . . . rave and beat." Such is its fury that it forces its way into the castle, making the lamp flicker, the arras sway and the carpets rise along the floor. There is an uproar without, and the tempest appears in the guise of an enemy laying siege. It is an agency hostile to mankind, actively at work.

That mysterious beings are lurking abroad has already been indicated by the lines:

> Never on such a night have lovers met,
> Since Merlin paid his Demon all the monstrous debt.

Indeed, for all the religious mood evoked by the title and the picture of the pious beadsman in the act of prayer, the poem has a sinister aspect which becomes more and more clearly visible in the course of the narrative. Thus Keats, trying to reinforce this suggestion of eerie peril, through Porphyro depicts the tumult in nature as "an elfin storm from faery land"—one that has been conjured up by supernatural power. The elves and fairies that wield this power are not to be thought of as the harmless, graceful creatures of *A Midsummer Night's Dream* but as kinsfolk of *La Belle Dame sans Merci*, herself a "faery's child" who dwelt in an "elfin grot" and wrought such woe that the dead rose to give warning against her.[1] The storm is "of haggard seeming," and, as Porphyro himself feels, wears an air of menace.

It is true that at the same time he perceives in it a convenient means of covering the escape, but his light-hearted ignorance is very likely meant as an example of tragic irony. Only a few stanzas earlier the poet has imparted a presentiment that all is not well. Madeline, seeing as she awakens the pallor of her lover, is seized with a sudden fear lest he should die:

> For if thou diest, my Love, I know not where to go.

On the assumption that both she and Porphyro are soon to perish together, Keats is here once more using tragic irony with marked effect.

Death is never far away in *The Eve of St. Agnes*. It appears imminent when Porphyro braves the "hyena foemen and hot-blooded lords," and in the midst of the vision scene the sound of the clarion and kettle-drum brings an admonition that mortal peril is near, while the flight of the lovers is pregnant with a sense of death in wait at every step. In this last passage the holograph version of the poem, which reads:

> The Lamps were flickering death shades on the walls
> Without, the Tempest kept a hollow roar,[2]

---

[1] In most of the poems into which Keats introduces fairies, they undoubtedly resemble those of Shakespeare. But the similarity is by no means uniform. In 1819 especially there are signs of independence in the *Song of Four Fairies*. There is too an indication in *Lamia* that fairies lent their aid in creating the illusion that ended so disastrously for Lycius, and in *La Belle Dame sans Merci* we again find a close connexion between the fairy world and the harm inflicted on human beings. In *The Eve of St. Agnes* there is nothing to define the nature of the "legion'd fairies" that "paced the coverlet" of Madeline, but the way in which the fairy people are mentioned in stanza xxxix is ominous.

[2] Stanza xl, 7–8. Cf. Keats, *The Poetical Works*, ed. H. B. Forman (Oxford, 1910), p. 228 and *The Poetical Works*, ed H. W. Garrod (Oxford, 1939), p. 255.

is still more deeply charged with this atmosphere than the printed
text. Through the secondary characters the same effect is conveyed.
The beadsman has hardly appeared when, we are told, "already
had his death-bell rung." Angela speaks of herself as one "whose
passing-bell may ere the midnight toll," and the main figures are
likewise touched by this breath from the grave when Madeline cries
aloud in sudden anxiety lest Porphyro should be snatched from
her. The closing stanza relates that in the course of the night both
Angela and the beadsman have passed away. So swiftly has what
was hinted at become reality. Is it not probable then that Keats,
working upon his readers indirectly, intended them to understand
that death overtook the lovers also? It is surely not fanciful to interpret the woe-filled dream of the Baron and the nightmare
visions

Of witch, and demon, and large coffin-worm

that haunted his warrior-guests as the unrest occasioned by the fate
of Porphyro and Madeline. The macabre grimness of the words
here used, closely akin in tone to the original first stanza of the
Ode on Melancholy, is startling, and the mention of witch and demon may be taken to imply that some baneful force is in motion,
the dangerous and malignant force already alluded to by Porphyro.
Obviously we are meant to realize that some dire calamity must
have occurred to beget such nightmares. They can certainly not
have been inspired by the loss of two aged retainers whose decease
was to be looked for at any moment. Yet insignificant as these
dependants are, one would not expect them to be treated with the
neglect that is the lot at any rate of the beadsman who

For aye unsought-for slept among his ashes cold.

Such indifference might be held to savour of callousness, but would
be more comprehensible if the death of the beadsman were lost
sight of in the major tragedy of the lovers.

However, quite apart from what can be gleaned from *The Eve
of St. Agnes* itself, the examination of other poems written by Keats
about the same time provides support for the view that it ends
tragically. Among those which repay scrutiny, as Professor L. C.
Martin points out, is the *Dream, after reading Dante's Episode of*

Paolo and Francesca, which was composed only a few weeks after the story of Porphyro and Madeline. In the *Inferno* Keats had read how

> La bufera infernal, che mai non resta,
> Mena gli spirti con la sua rapina,
> *Voltando* e *percotendo* li molesta.

The emphasis is on the incessant whirling and buffeting of the lovers by the wind, and nothing is said of cold and hailstones accompanying the "melancholy storm." Neither in the original nor in Cary's translation is there any hint of the exquisite sensations of Keats's dream—sensations united with a feeling of warmth amid the enveloping cold and darkness.[3] In all this there is a manifest prolongation of the mood of the vision scene in *The Eve of St. Agnes,* and if Dante's infernal storm has developed into

> the gust, the whirlwind, and *the flaw*
> *Of rain and hail-stones,*

the change is clearly to be connected with the description of the tempest in the earlier poem.[4] The storm-motive in the *Dream* is bound up with that of love, the short-lived bliss of Paolo and Francesca which ended in death and the anguish and torment of hell. In the same way *La Belle Dame sans Merci* takes as its theme the rapture of love, followed by disenchantment and ultimate death, and *Lamia* and *Isabella* deal with love abruptly terminated, just when happiness is unfolding. As a result of the hostility of Apollonius, Lamia is banished, and so sombre is Keats's mood that he also makes Lycius fall lifeless, whereas in the source of the poem, Burton's *Anatomy of Melancholy,* he survives the catastrophe. Lorenzo is murdered by the malice of the brothers, and Isabella dies of a broken heart. The death of Porphyro and Madeline, when

---

[3] Cf. Keats's letter to George and Georgiana Keats in April 1819: "I floated about the whirling atmosphere as it is described with a beautiful figure to whose lips mine were joined as it seem'd for an age—and in the midst of all this cold and darkness I was warm" (*Letters,* ed. M. B. Forman [Oxford, 1935], p. 326).

[4] Stanzas XXXVI–XXXVII. It is of interest to note that in the letter cited above (p. 324) Keats speaks of "a north wind blowing." It seems likely that the snowy background of *The Eve of St. Agnes* and the mingled rain and hailstones of the *Dream* were suggested by the periods in which they were written—the one in January and February, the other in April.

their love burnt most brightly, would therefore harmonize with the trend of Keats's thought as it is revealed in these contemporary poems. It may perhaps be objected that Keats would probably be explicit about the disaster that overtook the lovers, as he was in *Lamia* and *Isabella*. Yet this does not necessarily follow. He may well have decided to proceed as in *La Belle Dame sans Merci* by suggestion rather than definite statement.

Yet another consideration deserves to be weighed. That is the parallel between *The Eve of St. Agnes* and one of Keats's favourite plays, *Romeo and Juliet*. There is a general similarity in the situations confronting the two pairs of lovers. The fierce enmity of rival houses forms the background, and as Romeo ventured to the Capulet ball, so Porphyro enters the Baron's castle, just as the revelry and dancing are at their height. In addition, though the circumstances may differ somewhat, the foreboding of Madeline may be compared with the "ill-divining soul" of Juliet when she looks down at Romeo in the garden. It may well be that, consciously or unconsciously, Keats carried the parallel further. If *The Eve of St. Agnes* ends with the death of the lovers, as the poem itself and the treatment of similar themes elsewhere in Keats's work justify us in thinking, fate in the shape of the storm blasts the joy of these young people, even as it destroys that of Romeo and Juliet.

It would therefore appear that there are substantial reasons in favour of this exposition of Keats's meaning. And his own love for Fanny Brawne at the time when he wrote the group of poems that has been considered, in the midst of his batle with an untoward fate in the form of illness, would afford a psychological explanation of his repeated choice of the bliss of love thwarted by adverse events as a theme.

There can, of course, be no final answer to the problem under discussion. But there is every indication that *The Eve of St. Agnes,* like *Lamia, La Belle Dame sans Merci, The Eve of St. Mark* and Coleridge's *Christabel,* is rooted in the strange fascination of sinister magic and superstition.[5] If it be agreed that this magic brings *The Eve of St. Agnes* to a tragic close, this interpretation lends to the poem a deeper significance and emphasizes its coherence, structural unity and sense of design. With admirable skill Keats drops

[5] Cf. Keats's *Poems*, ed. E. de Sélincourt (London, 1905), pp. 525–6.

hints of the danger that threatens the lovers from mortal hands, but even more notable is the art with which he uses the forces of nature not only as portents, but, in conjunction with the magic of hostile supernatural powers, as the agents of disaster. By a series of subtle modulations the tension is heightened or relaxed, as under Keats's hand these perils are allowed to become more or less insistent. The opening, on a moonlit winter night, is peaceful, though not without a sense of foreboding. The tension increases when Porphyro steals into the castle. For a while the danger is forgotten after he enters Madeline's room. Yet even here uneasy reminders intrude, and before long the feeling of menace returns with still greater acuteness. The hero grows pale and cold, and simultaneously the moon wanes. Its setting is the signal for the unleashing of all the powers of darkness and the violence of the elements. From now on danger threatens in a continual crescendo. Breathlessly we follow the progress of the lovers down the stairs and out of the door. They escape from the inmates of the castle, but only to be engulfed in the storm. The climax is reached, and we know that Porphyro and Madeline are gone for ever. Then the emotion ebbs away, and the fate of Angela and the beadsman, linked as they are by the tale with the lovers in life and death, brings the poem to a close as quiet as its beginning. The tragedy of Porphyro and Madeline, so dramatic in its suspense, is over, and an austere calm descends. Death the omnipotent has come to young and old,[6] and "the weariness, the fever, and the fret" are ended. Thus *The Eve of St. Agnes* is conspicuous for the firmness with which the story is controlled from start to finish. In the verse tale as in the ode Keats had achieved that mastery of form which is the hallmark of his mature poetry.

[6] Though the way in which Keats expresses himself at the end of *The Eve of St. Agnes* about the sorrows and disasters of life is not identical with that in the *Ode to a Nightingale*, stanza III, ll. 3–6, there is an underlying similarity in his emotion, as he realizes the grievous destiny of young and old alike.

"The Eve of St. Agnes"

by Earl Wasserman

I

. . . Despite shifting critical standards, "The Eve of St. Agnes" has never been freed from the limitations imposed upon it by the Pre-Raphaelites, to whom it was a kind of prototype of the artistic realization that provides a heightening of consciousness, a more exciting experience than life itself. . . . " 'Load every rift' of your subject with ore," Keats wrote to Shelley[1]; and it has been assumed that "The Eve of St. Agnes" fulfills this doctrine by the density of its riches—its dark and yet gorgeous atmosphere of mediaevalism; the undeviating and spirited directness of its slim narrative; the plump synaesthetic and empathic imagery; the delicate enwrapping of warmth in chill, of quiet in revelry, of love in hate, of youth in age.

To re-examine these effects and the means whereby they are attained would now be a work of supererogation, for the readings of the poem have inevitably been colored by the Victorian discovery that it is a storehouse of narrative, descriptive, atmospheric, and prosodic techniques for building a poetic dream-world. Indeed, the number of such commentaries seems to indicate that Keats succeeded too well in those matters that belong to artistry. Even Fausset, whose study attempts to trace the evolution of Keats' philosophic mind, claims that the romance has "no other aim but the creation of sensuous beauty," and that if Keats' career had ended

---

" 'The Eve of St. Agnes' " by Earl Wasserman. From The Finer Tone (Baltimore: The Johns Hopkins Press, 1953), pp. 97–137. Reprinted by permission of Earl Wasserman and The Johns Hopkins Press. Abridged by permission of Professor Wasserman.

[1] August 16, 1820.

with the writing of this poem "there would have been every excuse for posterity's acceptance of him as a poet who sought beauty for beauty's sake rather than for truth's." [2] Apparently the corruscating ore packed into the rifts dazzles our attention until we are made careless of the fact that the subject of the poem is the "vast idea" which Keats said ever rolled before his vision.[3]

For it must be clear by now that Keats' most splendid imaginative experiences were one with his most profound conceptions and beliefs. What his imagination seized as beauty was, to him, the truth that is to come; and his poetry most often explores the relation of what we experience as beauty to what we intuit as truth. In this very fact lies the possibility for the ambivalent interpretations of his poetry as now sensuous, and now philosophic. Since sensuous experience is prefigurative of ultimate values in Keats' scheme of things, one may wrench out of their context the descriptive splendors and read either the philosophic meanings or the "gorgeous gallery of poetic pictures." But if we accept Keats' own premises concerning the relation of esthetic experience to metaphysical values, we are justified in adopting, at least as a working hypothesis, a belief that a high seriousness, an inner vision, inheres as much in "The Eve of St. Agnes" as it does in "La Belle Dame sans Merci."

II

It is most convenient to examine first the central episode of the romance, the union of Madeline and Porphyro, and then to analyze the larger surrounding units until the entire poem is encompassed. The justification for proceeding in this manner is the fact that the structure of the poem is a series of concentric circles that expand and deepen each other's meaning.

The most striking feature about the climax is the peculiar confusion of wake and sleep that characterizes Madeline's perception of Porphyro when she is being roused from her vision:

> Her eyes were open, but she still beheld,
> Now wide awake, the vision of her sleep. (298–99)

[2] *Keats, a Study in Development* (London, 1922), 70, 75.
[3] "Sleep and Poetry," 291.

We have already seen that in Keats' mind dreams are synonymous with imagination, for both are powers whereby man may penetrate into heaven's bourne, where the intensities of mortal life are repeated in a finer tone and divested of their mutability. Keats had linked sleep and poetry in the title of one of his early poems and there asked "what is higher beyond thought" than sleep. What, that is, brings us closer to heaven's bourne? . . .

Moreover, Madeline's dream does not take place in the ordinary course of mortal events but is occasioned by the mystical power of St. Agnes' Eve, when, by observing special rites, "Young virgins might have visions of delight" (47). It is a "hallow'd hour" (66), an extraordinary condition that, being outside the normal framework of experience, permits the imagination to rise to supernatural heights and correspondingly to penetrate most deeply into the beauty-truth that is to come. If dreams are imaginative visions of a future reality, St. Agnes' dreams are "the sweetest of the year" (63).

The relation of dream-visions to the imagination, and the manner in which they both function, were most clearly stated by Keats in a famous letter to Bailey.[4] "I am certain of nothing," he wrote,

> but of the holiness of the Heart's affections and the truth of Imagination—What the imaginaion seizes as Beauty must be truth—whether it existed before or not. . . . The Imagination may be compared to Adam's dream—he awoke and found it truth.

The reference is to that passage in *Paradise Lost* in which Adam tells of the creation of Eve. . . . God had fulfilled his pledge to Adam to realize "Thy wish, exactly to thy heart's desire." Now, by making of Adam's dream in Eden a parable of the imagination Keats certainly did not mean that we shall know in our mortal careers that our imaginings are true; here we can know only a beauty that must die, but in awakening into the reality to come we shall discover that the extraordinary imaginative insights we experience here will hereafter be experienced under the conditions of immortality. Our earthly visions of an Eve, who is our heart's desire, the essence of all the beauty that earth or heaven can be-

[4] November 22, 1817.

stow or our imaginations fashion, will hereafter be enjoyed as immutable realities. But Keats felt a conviction that this heaven of immortal passion can be entered only through an intensity of experience in this life, only by a mystic entrance into the essence of that beauty which here fades; for we shall each be allotted an immortality of that degree of passion that our earthly careers have attained. Therefore,

> O for a Life of Sensations rather than of Thoughts! It is "a Vision in the form of Youth" a Shadow of reality to come—and this consideration has further convinced me for it has come as auxiliary to another favorite Speculation of mine, that we shall enjoy ourselves here after by having what we called happiness on Earth repeated in a finer tone and so repeated. And yet such a fate can only befall those who delight in Sensation rather than hunger as you do after Truth. Adam's dream will do here and seems to be a conviction that Imagination and its empyreal reflection is the same as human Life and its Spiritual repetition.

Briefly, a life of sensations provides us with experiences of beauty that we shall later enjoy under those immortal conditions that Keats called "truth"; it foreshadows in the transitory the "reality" to come. . . .

When, therefore, Madeline is awakened from her divine vision, her capacity to perceive both human life and the spiritual repetition of it that her transcendent dream has divulged allows her to experience simultaneously both the mortal and the immortal. Ideally, this sensory-visionary state should correspond to the nature of heaven's bourne, where the human and the ethereal, beauty and truth, are one. The mortal Porphyro presented to her senses and the ideal Porphyro of her vision should fuse mystically into an immortality of passionate experience, as warmly human as the one and yet as immutable as the other. . . . [But] the difference between the mortal Porphyro and the visionary Porphyro—human life and its spiritual repetition—is too great to allow the two to coalesce into a human–ethereal identity; and consequently the sight of mortality was to Madeline "a painful change, that nigh expell'd / The blisses of her dream so pure and deep" (300–301). In her vision of immortality Porphyro's eyes were "spiritual and clear," but now she finds them "sad," sadness being inextricable from

human existence. "How chang'd thou art! how pallid, chill, and
drear!" she adds (311), for Porphyro, like the knight-at-arms and
his fellow mortals, is death-pale with the pallor, chill, and dreari-
ness inherent in the nature of mortality. . . .

Madeline's dream, then, is Adam's—but her awakening is, for
the moment, far different. By spiritual grace she has experienced
in a finer tone what she has called happiness on earth. And yet, she
has not awakened from her dream to find it truth, for in the
mutable world into which she is awakening, beauty is not truth,
passions are not immortal, eyes are not spiritual and clear. Only
in heaven's bourne do men of sensations awaken to find that their
empyreal imaginings are true. Hence Madeline is being called back
to an existence that is necessarily sorrowful and to a world where
every knight-at-arms is "woe-begone." The impending dissolution
of her vision through the summons to mutability and decay causes
her to

weep,
And moan forth witless words with many a sigh;
While still her gaze on Porphyro would keep.   (302–304)

In one sense, then, Madeline's double vision is an analogue of a
heaven's bourne that for the moment refuses to come about because
her ideal dream and her sensory perception refuse to coalesce. But
in another sense Madeline is herself the ideal and coldly chaste
steadfastness of the bright star which, when animated with an
exquisite intensity of warm human passion, becomes the oxymo-
ronic nature of life's spiritual repetition.[5] For the magic of St.
Agnes' Eve has transformed her into a Cynthia, the completed form
of all completeness. In her chastity, her visionary power, and the
spiritual purity that St. Agnes' Eve has bestowed upon her, she is
the immutability of the life to come, but not its human intensity.
She is "St. Agnes' charmed maid" (192), "a mission'd spirit"
(193), "all akin / To spirits of the air" (201–202), "so pure a thing,
so free from mortal taint" (225); she seems a saint, "a splendid
angel, newly drest, / Save wings, for heaven" (222–24). Caught up
in her dream-vision, she is sheltered alike from joy and pain (240),
those complementary passions that attend upon all man's experi-

---

[5] "Bright star! would I were steadfast as thou art."

ences while he is on earth. In withdrawing into her own self in sleep she becomes the perfection of form, "As though a rose should shut, and be a bud again" (243); she is not the full-blown rose giving up its fragrance, just as living is an expenditure of life, but a self-contained and unexpended power with need of nothing beyond itself, an emblem of Becoming eternally captured, and therefore perfect and immutable. Consequently, the merely human Porphyro worships her as his "heaven," while he sees himself as her "eremite" (277). She is, in short, the condition of immortality at heaven's bourne, its freedom from time, space, and selfhood.

But at heaven's bourne love is not simply forever *to be* enjoyed; it is not immutable simply because it is never experienced. It is at the same time forever *being* enjoyed. And it is the human Porphyro, not graced by the supernal power of St. Agnes' Eve, who is the human passion that Madeline will raise to an immortality. He must so "delight in Sensation" that a "Spiritual repetition" of his earthly happiness will be available to him. . . .

In the poem, therefore, a miracle is to be performed; and instead of being thrust back into humanity after the "many hours of toil and quest" (338) which make up man's effort to become one with his ideal and to achieve an identity of truth and beauty, Porphyro will succeed in order that the mystery into which man would thereby penetrate may be revealed. For this purpose he is "A famish'd pilgrim,—saved by miracle" (339). Since only an intensity of passion can lead to a future repetition in a finer tone of what we call happiness on earth, and since such a repetition is permitted only to one who delights in sensations, Porphyro must first arise "Beyond a mortal man impassion'd far" (316). The ambiguous syntax (Keats first wrote, "Impassioned far beyond a mortal man") implies that Porphyro's passion remains human in its nature and yet is raised to superhuman intensity. Only in this manner can the gap between mortal and immortal be bridged, for Porphyro thereby is raising human passion to the "finer tone" in which it will be experienced hereafter. In this act Porphyro has become "ethereal" (318). The word, we have seen, is a favorite with Keats and usually describes the transfiguration of real things into values by means of ardor. By the straining of his passion

Porphyro has become an "ethereal thing," a value that is the ultimate significance of his mortal self and its experiences. Now, and
only now, beauty may be united with truth, the mortal with the
ethereal, to become the eternity of passion that exists only in
heaven's bourne:

> Ethereal, flush'd, and like a throbbing star
> Seen mid the sapphire heaven's deep repose
> Into her dream he melted, as the rose
> Blendeth its odour with the violet,—
> Solution sweet.   (318–22)

The steadfastness of the bright star and the soft fall and swell of
"love's ripening breast" have coalesced; or rather, to use the images of the stanza, the throbbing of the star has been absorbed
into the repose of the sky. The mortal Porphyro has risen to such
a degree of passionate ardor that it may now blend with the chaste
immutability that Madeline has become by virtue of the grace of
St. Agnes' Eve. By the blending of their powers Madeline and
Porphyro are now experiencing the spiritual repetition of human
life and can therefore move into its mystery. . . . Madeline's dream
has turned out to be Adam's after all; by a miracle she has awakened to find it truth.

While this immortality of passion is dramatically evolving in the
foreground through the overt actions which melt the human ardor
of Porphyro into the ideal constancy, the "deep repose," of Madeline's vision, a parallel development is also taking place in the
background which not only infuses into the central drama a powerful tonal quality but also re-enacts symbolically the union of Porphyro and Madeline so as to expand the otherwise personal action
to cosmic size and significance. Waiting to be led to Madeline,
Porphyro remains in "a little moonlight room, / Pale, lattic'd,
chill, and silent as a tomb" (112–13). There Angela tells him of
Madeline's intention to observe the rites of St. Agnes' Eve, and as
a result

> Sudden a thought came like a full-blown rose,
> Flushing his brow, and in his pained heart
> Made purple riot.   (136–38)

These two symbols—cold and silvery pale moonlight, and the warmly sensuous ruddiness of purple and rose—correspond to the two conditions that are one in heaven's bourne. In the first room Porphyro is in the presence of the moonlight, but it is only lifeless and chill unless it is animated by the color of passion, the roseate sensuousness that at length is born in Porphyro. Silver and moonlight therefore hover about Madeline, the Cynthia of the poem, the eternal form with which human passion must blend. She carries "a silver taper" (194) which dies in the "pallid moonshine" of her own chamber (200); she wears a silver cross (221); and before Keats finally described her as a "splendid angel" (223) he tried "immortal angel" and "silvery angel." She is Porphyro's "silver shrine" (337), he her beauty's shield, "heart-shap'd and vermeil dyed" (336).

The silveriness and moonlight belong to the realm of pure being, the rich blushes of color to the realm of passionate becoming. Consequently, when Madeline enters her chamber the two colors begin to run together, interpenetrating to prefigure the act which will coalesce human and spiritual into a love that is "still to be enjoy'd." The chaste moonlight shines through the stained-glass windows, whose gorgeous colors are "Innumerable of stains and splendid dyes, / As are the tiger-moth's deep-damask'd wings" (212–13) so that the two colors partake of each other as though cosmic forces had shaped at an all-pervasive level the heaven's bourne that Madeline and Porphyro are to find at the human level. In this silver-red, or chaste-sensuous atmosphere fusion, the subsequent action of the spirit-sense union is bathed. The cold, virginal light of the "wintry moon" throws a warm roseate stain on Madeline's white breast; it makes rose-bloom fall on her hands, which are clasped in holy prayer; it covers the silvery spirituality of her cross with the luxurious purple of amethyst (217–21).

The fusion continues to permeate the setting as Porphyro prepares for the union. In the "dim, silver twilight" he places a cloth of "woven crimson, gold, and jet" (253–56); he fills with fruit golden dishes and baskets of "wreathed silver" (271–73); and lustrous salvers gleaming in the moonlight and golden-fringed carpets appear as adjacent images (284–85). As the bloody dyes have become the sensuous vitality of the virginal moonlight, Porphyro now rises to ethereal passions to melt into Madeline's spiritual vision. The scents of the rose and the chaste violet dissolve into each other (320–22). The union having been consummated and the conditions of heaven's bourne having been attained, the supernatural grace is no longer needed or pertinent. Porphyro and Madeline have fashioned their own heaven: "St. Agnes' moon hath set" (324).

III

As the poem was passing through its various manuscript forms, Keats added and later deleted a stanza between what are now stanzas six and seven. Stanza six describes some of the ceremonies required of virgins on St. Agnes' Eve if they are to have their visions of delight, and the deleted stanza then added:

> 'Twas said her future lord would there appear
> Offering as sacrifice—all in the dream—
> Delicious food even to her lips brought near:
>
> Viands and wine and fruit and sugar'd cream,
> To touch her palate with the fine extreme
> Of relish: then soft music heard; and then
> More pleasures followed in a dizzy stream
> Palpable almost: then to wake again
> Warm in the virgin morn, no weeping Magdalen.

Had the stanza been retained, the reader would be better prepared for Porphyro's otherwise unmotivated actions in Madeline's chamber and for some of Angela's bustlings. But even so, the critic would have been required to face the problems the stanza introduces. Almost uniformly the commentators have agreed with William Michael Rossetti on the irrelevance of the feast later in the poem: "One of the few subsidiary incidents introduced into 'The Eve of St. Agnes' is that the lover Porphyro, on emerging from his hiding-place while his lady is asleep, produces from a cupboard and marshals to sight a large assortment of appetizing eatables. Why he did this no critic and no admirer has yet been able to divine." [6] Most significant, the omitted stanza outlines the only important action Porphyro engages in prior to his union with Madeline, except for his passage from one chamber to another. Even if these otherwise irrelevant actions concerning food and music were requirements of the legend, as Keats pretends, why does he give them such significance in a narrative remarkable for its unilinear direction? Why, when the other rituals are only lightly touched upon, does Keats have Angela speak particularly of the food and the lute? and why does he then dwell upon these two rituals when Porphyro is in Madeline's chamber?

But, in fact, the details outlined in the omitted stanza have not been found to be part of the legend. The folk tradition does require that the virgin lie supine, look not behind her, speak not a word, retire fasting, and look to heaven for aid; however, there is no evidence that it requires a feast and music. We must search, instead, for some compelling reason why Keats introduced more than the narrative itself calls for. Once again, it is clear, he has reshaped a legend in order to weave through it the series of increasing intensities of the pleasure thermometer that he understood to be the necessary means of spiritual elevation before one may enter the dynamically static heaven Madeline and Porphyro are about to create for themselves. The rich foods correspond to the level of sensuous essence, and Keats is careful to underscore the sensory vigor he means to convey: "To touch her palate with the fine extreme / Of relish." Then music; and at last, since the subject has now stepped into "a sort of oneness," the great range of "happinesses" made up of love and friendship. These essences are to be so strenuously envisioned that they are "Palpable almost"— sensuous and yet spiritual, real and yet visionary, beautiful and yet true.

We can now understand why, after Porphyro has told Angela his plan to enact physically the visions of Madeline's dreams—that is, to perform in human reality what Madeline is experiencing at a transcendent level—Angela is quick to reply:

> "It shall be as thou wishest . . .
> "All cates and dainties shall be stored there

[6] *Life of John Keats* (London, 1887), 183.

the ballance of good and evil. We are in a Mist. *We* are now in that state—We feel the "burden of the Mystery." To this Point was Wordsworth come, as far as I can conceive when he wrote "Tintern Abbey" and it seems to me that his Genius is explorative of those dark Passages. Now if we live, and go on thinking, we too shall explore them.[7]

The stages outlined here correspond roughly to the three implicit in "Tintern Abbey": a period of thoughtless animal pleasure without even awareness of the pleasure, one of consciousness of emotional power, and at last a perception of the "still, sad music of humanity" which brings a sense of "something far more deeply interfused" and consequently lightens "the burden of the mystery." The relation Keats' letter has to Wordsworth's pattern of life and of the growth of the poetic mind reveals how deeply indebted Keats was to the older poet for his own most profound inquiry into the meaning of human existence.

In the career of Porphyro, then, Keats has incorporated his semi-Wordsworthian vision of life as a progress from mere animal existence to an understanding of the mystery that permeates life; and the castle is that Mansion of Many Apartments in which human existence plays out its part. When Porphyro arrives at the castle he stands beside the portal doors, "Buttress'd from moonlight" (77), merely hoping that he may gaze on Madeline, the beauty for which he longs. In this infant existence of his spirit, he is shut off from the light of the ideal moon which shines on mortal things to reveal them in their immortal aspects; and consequently in the "tedious hours" (79) which make up life he can do no more than yearn for an entrance into existence so as to experience its riches: "Perchance speak, kneel, touch, kiss" (80–81). . . .

But this worldly beauty toward which he is impelled before he enters the castle is not transfigured by the spiritual light of the moon-goddess, and hence he has no understanding of the meaning of his impulse. However, having entered the castle of human life, he quickly circumvents the level chambers of the "mansion foul" (89) in which life is a distracting game played for its own sake and where the "barbarian hordes" resent all that he represents. Led

---

[7] Letter to Reynolds, May 3, 1818.

by Angela to the first chamber, he is there bathed in the light of
ideality, but, since the intensity of human passion is lacking, the
room is only "Pale, lattic'd, chill, and silent as a tomb" (113).
In this "thoughtless Chamber, in which we remain as long as we
do not think," Porphyro merely exists, resting in childlike innocence and awe, "Like puzzled urchin," while Angela tells of Madeline's plan. In this spiritual adolescence he is driven by an impulse
of his senses, but not by a consciousnes of his sensuous desires.
Angela's revelation, however, arouses him from the thoughtlessness
which allows him to remain in the first chamber, and knowledge
of Madeline's intention to experience the spiritual repetition of
earthly happiness awakens the thinking principle within him and
impels him to seek out Madeline's chamber: "Sudden a thought
came like a full-blown rose, . . . then doth he propose / A
stratagem" (136–39). The consciousness of his sensuous powers
drives him then to Madeline's chamber—the "Chamber of Maiden-
Thought."

The spiritual ascent that is implicit in Porphyro's progress from
chamber to chamber becomes clear by the fact that he remains
in a closet adjacent to Madeline's chamber, for Keats originally
called this closet a "Purgatory sweet" and retained his description
of the chamber itself as a "paradise." In other words, Porphyro
has transcended the merely human life of the "level chambers"
and is now in the purgatory to which he must move before he
can attain the heavenly repetition of earthly happiness. From this
purgatory he can look upon "all that he may attain," "love's own
domain." [8] In the Chamber of Maiden-Thought we are intoxicated
with the light and atmosphere and see nothing but pleasant
wonders; and thus Porphyro looks upon the disrobing Madeline,
the ideal revealing its naked perfection. . . . Here in the Chamber
of Maiden-Thought the ascent of the scale of intensities is acted
out, and Porphyro and Madeline unite in a mystic blending of
mortality and immortality, chastity and passion, the moonlight of
perfect form and the ruddiness of intense experience. They have
attained the stage where life's self is nourished by its own pith,
and they can now progress into the mystery that is the core of
life. . . .

[8] Stanza 21, variant.

Having experienced the spiritual repetition of human happiness, Porphyro and Madeline are no longer active powers. Of his friend Dilke, Keats wrote that he will never arrive at a truth because he is always striving after it[9]; and Coleridge, he complained, will "let go by a fine isolated verisimilitude caught from the Penetralium of mystery, from being incapable of remaining Content with half knowledge." [10] One enters the mystery, not by wilfull probing, but by allowing himself to be absorbed into it. Once man has experienced the wonders of the Chamber of Maiden-Thought and gained insight into the agony of human life, the mystery unfolds itself; and an effort to pry open its doors would only shut them more tightly. Therefore, in the poem the light grows dark, and the mystery opens its own doors upon itself: "on all sides of it," as the letter to Reynolds says, "many doors are set open.". . .

With the enactment of this theme of passive absorption Keats now rounds out the conclusion of his romance. In one of the most dramatically controlled passages in English poetry he melts the lovers into a spaceless, timeless, selfless realm of mystery, exactly as the poet of the "Ode on a Grecian Urn" and the knight-at-arms were selflessly assimilated into a visionary heaven. At first we perceive the lovers preparing to escape into the storm that lies beyond human existence; they themselves are the object of our attention as we see them moving down the wide stairs. They act directly before us in the historical past. Then, almost imperceptibly they are gradually released from dimensions. First they tend to fade as active powers. After having been vividly active before us and the center of our attention, they govern little directly in the last three stanzas; in the main the action passes from them into the control of the things that surround them—the lamp, arras, carpets, bloodhound, chains, key, and door; and the sense of their active presence is further dimmed by the introduction of the passive verb: "In all the house was heard no human sound" (356).

They further lose selfhood and palpable existence as the reader becomes identified with them, moving in them through the passageways and seeing, no longer the lovers, but what could be seen by

---

[9] Letter to George and Georgiana Keats, September 17–27, 1819.
[10] Letter to George and Thomas Keats, December 21, 1817.

them in their progress—the flickering of the lamp, the fluttering of the arras, the rising of the carpets with the wind. The camera is no longer focused on the lovers, but has become their eyes so that as we watch what the lovers see, they themselves may steal away from our mode of existence. When next we glance at them they have become indistinct and have blurred into insubstantial things; their movement is the insubstantial essence of movement, not a human act, and they themselves have become visionary. . . .

All human agency also vanishes as the lovers fade entirely from the scene. We do not see them as they make the bolts of the castle door slide open, nor are we the lovers seeing their own action of moving the bolts; for the effect of one's arrival at the border of the mystery is that "many doors *are set* open." No agency at all slides the bolts and chains, and yet the bolts and chains slide, and the door groans on its hinges—and Porphyro and Madeline are outside the human order, beyond the "mysterious doors" that lead to "universal knowledge." The lovers are wholly caught up in timelessness and no longer exist as human actors. "And they are gone": the action of the participle ("gone") belongs to the past, but the adjectival use of the participle here divests it of its verbal quality; it is a description, a quality of being, not an act, and therefore it implies no agency. The lovers' being gone is outside time and activity. The poet now catches up this sense of timelessness and swells it by having endless ages spin away before our time-bound minds:

> And they are gone: ay, ages long ago
> These lovers fled away into the storm. (370–71)

No longer are Porphyro and Madeline human actors, or even phantoms, but the selfless spirit of man forever captured in the dimensionless mystery beyond our mortal vision. . . .

V

In the background of the narrative we have been tracing there are three other sets of characters who, by their contrast with the warmth, passion, and ardor of the youthful lovers, not only give the central narrative an artistic depth, but also act out their various roles in the Mansion of Many Apartments to reveal other ways in which life may be lived. The beadsman, who surrounds the entire poem with a framework of chill, plays his part in the outer passages of the castle. . . . He leads his mortal life only that he may put it aside; by praying for his soul's reprieve and grieving for sinners' sake he hopes to stifle his physical existence and thereby exalt and assure his spiritual salvation.

But the enjoyment in a finer tone hereafter of what we have called happiness on earth is a fate that "can only befall those who delight in Sensation rather than hunger as you do after Truth," Keats wrote to his clerical friend Benjamin Bailey.[11] Adam's dream does not apply to those who, like the beadsman, hunger after "truth." Even the beadsman's breath symbolizes the misdirection of his life: his breath (spirit) "Seem'd taking flight for heaven, without a death" (8). But death, Keats tells us elsewhere, is "Life's high meed" [12]—the final intensity that climaxes the intensities of human existence and unites life with its proper pith. For the man of sensations, human experiences are a progress to heaven's bourne, and death is the last and most vigorous of these experiences.

The beadsman's, however, is "Another way" (25); he hopes, not to make sensuous earthly existence an ascent to a spiritual repetition, but to dodge life and its high meed, death, and to be as oblivious to the senses as his fingers are numb with the cold. He would grasp "truth" alone, without beauty, in one leap. For such a life which avoids sensations there is no spiritual repetition in a finer tone; and the beadsman, after thousand futile aves, becomes only the mutable physical substance that belongs to this world: "For aye unsought for slept among his ashes cold" (378). The irony is that on the very night that the lovers are caught up in the mystery through the fixing of exquisite passion in an immortality, the beadsman, seeking to subdue the flesh to the spirit, becomes only meaningless, lifeless matter among the very ashes that symbolize the meaninglessness of the mortal body. . . .

And yet, the revelers in the hall, the converse of the beadsman, cannot perceive beyond the limits of their momentary excitement. In the "level chambers" they seek pleasure and agitation merely

---

[11] Letter to Bailey, November 22, 1817.
[12] "Why did I laugh to-night?"

as an end in itself. . . . Thus the beadsman and the baron's guests are antitheses: the first avoids life for soul; the latter neglect soul for life alone. For this very reason the beadsman is irrelevant to the lovers and moves about the periphery of the castle; but the baron and his guests are hostile to them. . . . The revelers engage in only the petty passions of the world: "whisperers in anger, or in sport; / 'Mid looks of love, defiance, hate, and scorn" (68–9); and only because "her heart was otherwhere" (62) could Madeline fulfill the rites of St. Agnes' Eve and experience the spiritual repetition of life. . . .

For this life of the senses alone, Keats cannot restrain his contempt. The "barbarian hordes" are "bloated wassaillers" (346) who, being "Drown'd all in Rhenish and the sleepy mead," do not have "ears to hear, or eyes to see" the passage of the lovers from the castle of mortality into the mystery of the elfin storm (348–49). Consequently, the dreams of the baron and his guests—"the whole blood-thirsty race" (99)—unlike Madeline's dream, are only of the world in which all things decay. Instead of rising by dream-vision to the spiritual repetition of human life, they can dream only of human life, whose central principle is its deathliness:

> That night the Baron dreamt of many a woe,
> And all his warrior-guests, with shade and form
> of witch, and demon, and large coffin-worm,
> Were long be-nightmar'd. (372–75)

Finally, both the drama and the theme of the poem are completed by Angela, who is a kind of norm of humanity. Like the beadsman, she is careful of her soul; and yet she belongs to the halls of revelry rather than the higher chambers, although she alone is able to wander at will in both, unaffected by either. She will never experience a love that is forever warm and still to be enjoyed because she is devoid of both sensuous and spiritual intensity: she is an "old beldame, weak in body and in soul" (90), a "poor, weak, palsy-stricken, churchyard thing" (155). Madeline's desire for a vision of her love is to Angela only a child's wish for an unreal, deceptive dream-world. . . .

Although she aids in Porphyro's enactment of the vision, the part she plays is almost too exacting for her feeble spirit and senses.

She rises to a height beyond her strength, and so Madeline must lead her from the upper chambers down "To a safe level matting" (196), the level at which merely human existence is carried on and at which the baron and his guests seek worldly happiness. Since such weakness can never penetrate into the mystery, Angela, whose "passing-bell may ere the midnight toll" (156), on the very same night (we are left to assume) died "palsy-twitch'd, with meagre face deform" (375–76).

VI

It is, of course, a great convenience that we have Keats' letter on the Mansion of Many Apartments, for it is an elucidation of Porphyro's progress almost detail by detail. And yet, having made use of it, I should like to remove it from all considerations of the poem as poem. . . . For "The Eve of St. Agnes" is a self-contained poetic cosmos; it is symbolic, not allegorical. The beadsman is not to be translated as Christian asceticism; he is that asceticism. The union of Porphyro and Madeline does not stand for anything, but is in itself the mystic oxymoron which is heaven. . . . Man, not God, is the etherealizer, the symbolizer. And yet, a human life of sensations is itself symbolic, for such a life etherealizes itself through its own ardor and thus becomes a symbol of values. The basis of this belief is Keats' assumption that the intense experiences of life and the values which make them intelligible are different degrees of the same thing. Since "we shall enjoy ourselves here after by having what we called happiness on Earth repeated in a finer tone," and since all values reside in this spiritual repetition, then the sensations of human life are prefigurative of these values and are causally related to them. Hence the life of sensations is symbolic because it creates its own hereafter and consequently its own meaning. . . .

Because of Keats' basic premise, the life of sensations cannot be other than a temporal foreshadowing of the eternal and partake of the reality which it renders intelligible. Indeed, it creates that reality, for each man's existence in eternity is a spiritual re-enactment of his temporal happiness, and intensity of experience will cause human life to partake of its own spiritual core, that essence in which all values are to be found. Therefore the climax of Porphyro's career is his etherealizing of himself through the superlative degree of his sensations (318), his self-elevation into a symbol; it is at this point that his existence has taken on a value, and is becoming a living part of that unity of which it is the representative.

The man of sensations, then, is the symbolizer. . . . The "life of any worth," it is clear, must be a life of sensations; and its mystery, of which it is figurative, is the spiritual re-enactment which it makes possible. Such a life is both itself and part of that ultimate reality it renders intelligible. What the artist does is to live this life of worth and to capture its meaning, its spiritual repetition, in his art. Art, therefore, is a mode of representing in its finer tone the life of sensations. And "The Eve of St. Agnes" is a special enactment of such a life—like Shakespeare's plays, a comment on it.

"The Eve of St. Agnes"

by Bernard Blackstone

The Eve of St. Agnes is, in a sense, Keats's own answer to Isabella. The earlier poem had been a tragedy of kinship; St. Agnes is a narrative of kinship with a happy ending. Isabella had culminated in the frustration of a biological destiny; St. Agnes carries to a triumphant conclusion an adventure of romantic daring. Isabella had diverted Keats from his main current; in St. Agnes he returns to it.

The poem's movement is precisely antithetical to that of Isabella. There, the flow was from life to death, from the specious promise of "great happiness" growing "like a lusty flower in June's caress" to the "wintry cold" of the forest tomb. Nature's purposes are thwarted: "those dainties made to still an infant's cries" are "frozen utterly unto the bone." Wintry images, together with "marble tombs," dying plants, decay, and mournful music, throng its concluding stanzas. In St. Agnes the tombs are initial: we move rapidly from the "bitter chill" of "sculptur'd dead" seeming to freeze "emprison'd in black, purgatorial rails" to "the poppied warmth" of Madeline's slumber and the luxuriant pyramids of fruit and spices

> heap'd with glowing hand
> On golden dishes and in baskets bright
> Of wreathed silver.

The movement is vertical: we journey with Porphyro from the darkness and cold of the grave (which is also the place of the seed and the root) into the warmth and fragrance of the nuptial chamber (the place of flowering and fruition). All in all, we can say that St.

"'The Eve of St. Agnes'" by Bernard Blackstone. From The Consecrated Urn (London: Longmans Green & Co. Ltd., 1959), pp. 275–88. Reprinted by permission of Longmans Green & Co. Ltd.

Agnes constitutes a new manifesto for Keats—more assured, more compact and more finished than *Endymion*—of faith in his own powers, of trust in those "great allies" the rhythms of the seasons and the blessedly steadfast, impersonal forces of nature; and above all, perhaps, it is a pæan of rejoicing in the flowering of his love for Fanny Brawne, and the love she gave him in return.

In *Endymion* the rigours of winter, as we have seen, were omitted from the picture. The development of the poem, which Keats intended initially to integrate with the course of his own life from April to October 1817,[1] must close with autumn:

> O may no wintry season, bare and hoary,
> See it half-finish'd; but let Autumn bold,
> With universal tinge of sober gold,
> Be all about me when I make an end.

In *Isabella* the season is introduced in a simile. But at last, in the *Eve,* Keats comes to close grips with winter. It is a sign of his own development, of his growing acceptance of life's darker aspects.[2] An acceptance which is not a surrender, but involves their mastery and their transmutation. The static quality of *Isabella* has disappeared. The new poem is instinct with that energy by which principles pressed to their extreme suffer dramatic reversal. We noted this "dialectic" in the Cave of Quietude episode of *Endymion*. It is evident again in two sonnets of early 1818: the one, *To Homer,* stresses darkness:

> Aye, on the shores of darkness there is light,
> And precipices show untrodden green;
> There is a budding morrow in midnight;
> There is a triple sight in blindness keen;

the other, untitled, stresses both darkness and winter:

> O thou whose face hath felt the Winter's wind,
> Whose eye has seen the snow-clouds hung in mist,

---

[1] Keats was a month out in his reckoning: the poem was not finished until near the end of November. But he had already "revoked" the promise in *Letters,* 29.

[2] And of course of life's basic rhythm too. It is in the sonnet "Four seasons fill the measure of the year" of September 1818 that he admits of man: "He has his Winter too of pale misfeature, Or else he would forego his mortal nature."

> And the black elm tops 'mong the freezing stars,
> To thee the spring will be a harvest-time.
> O thou, whose only book has been the light
>   Of supreme darkness which thou feddest on
>   Night after night when Phœbus was away,
> To thee the Spring shall be a triple morn.

Into his basic pattern of growth, flowering and fruition Keats is now learning to integrate the essential, though seemingly negative, element of immobility, darkness, and cold. The richness of *St. Agnes' Eve* derives, as we shall see, from this integration.

The poem develops by dramatic contrasts. Throughout the first three stanzas we are, to all intents and purposes, in the grave. The Beadsman, crouched "among rough ashes" in his crypt, is more dead than alive—"already had his deathbell rung." He is encompassed by images of death.[3] Cold and darkness triumph. Then, abruptly, the silence is broken by the blare of trumpets "up aloft." We ascend to another level of this microcosm which is the storm-beaten castle among the moors. We move from the "mineral" realm to the "vegetable": to the plane of mechanical enjoyment, of noise and laughter and bustle:

> At length burst in the argent revelry,
> With plume, tiara, and all rich array,
> Numerous as shadows haunting fairily
> The brain, new stuff'd, in youth, with triumphs gay
> Of old romance.[4]

As the poem stands Keats's intention is far from clear. The revellers are shadows, yes: but how are we to think of them? In some omitted lines we find the answer:

> Ah what are they? the idle pulse scarce stirs
> The Muse should never make the spirit gay;
> Away, bright dulness, laughing fools away—

---

[3] Cf. Darwin, *The Loves of the Plants*, III, 19–30, for some odd "Mother Radcliffe" parallels with this and other parts of *St. Agnes* and *St. Mark*. We find much the same locus and atmosphere in Pope's *Eloisa to Abelard* (cf. especially lines 17–24 and 303–308).

[4] Such, indeed, as had haunted Keats's own brain. *St. Agnes* is the poem to which the *Specimen of an Induction* (c. 1816) is prefatory. *Calidore*, the second Gothic fragment in *Poems 1817*, gives us the "trumpet's silver voice" (line 55) which will sound again in *St. Agnes* and *Lamia*.

Life lived on the purely sensual level—which is also the social level, so that Keats's later anguish about Fanny Brawne is anticipated here—is unworthy of the Muse. We turn away from the bright surface which conceals such depths of dullness, to Madeline, whose thoughts are of love. Here our progress is still upwards, to the human level, with its possibilities of transformation under "the fairy power Of unreflecting love." Madeline incarnates the power of a single emotion firmly conceived and held to create a new situation. She is the radiant centre of the microcosm, protected from trivial assault by the one-pointedness of his vision—

> . . . in vain
> Came many a tiptoe, amorous cavalier,
> And back retir'd

—yet attracting by the same concentration the one person necessary for her completion. Porphyro crosses the moors and enters the castle.

I have represented the process of the poem as a movement upwards through the three worlds. Rather more concretely, within the same framework, it might be represented as a plant with root, leaves and flowers. The root remains in the darkness below. It is cold and immobile. But it is not functionless. The Beadsman spends his hours in prayer for the inhabitants of the castle. He affords, that is, nourishment, and makes possible the final ripening of the golden fruit of love. Above the surface we see the leaves spreading. The "level chambers" of the castle are "ready with their pride." The leaves too are essential; but they are sterile; they do not flower. From among them there rises the single blossom, Madeline.

The above interpretation is, I believe, valid; but it should not be pushed too far or stressed exclusively. It is valid in that it "explains" the poem from one point of view, and because it helps us to integrate the poem with the corpus of Keats's growth and fruition symbolism. But there is another part of his symbolism which is just as basic: the hermetic-magical. Not that the two are radically separate. On the contrary, it is the vitalism in hermetic thought that attracted Keats. It is the sense of "no frontiers" in magic, and the sense of growth, of power, in contrast to the empirical philosophy's sterile restriction, that held his interest.

St. Agnes' Eve belongs to a group of poems, including *Isabella* and *St. Mark's Eve,* that exploit the same central situation: the appearance of a ghostly lover to a waiting girl. This situation is a supernatural one; and from this point of view we can place the group within a still wider group, written between April 1818 and September 1819, which are all poems of spell-binding or transformation. The series begins with *Isabella,* and ends with *Lamia.* We can say something else about these poems; they are all love-poems, and they explore the love-relationhip from various angles. The approach in *Isabella* is sentimental, and in *Lamia* cynical.

In *St. Agnes' Eve* the approach is "romantic," to use that word in the sense most commonly given it. When we talk of "romantic love" we mean the passion of which Keats's poem is a brilliant expression. It is "unreflecting love," but it is not "biological" or instinctive in the sense that the love of Isabella and Lorenzo was. The young mother note is not sounded. What is sounded is the religious note: and this is perhaps what we mean when we speak of romantic love. The same note rings in *Romeo and Juliet.* The girl is a saint, and the lover is her eremite. Love is their religion, and they need no other. Their love is an end in itself.[5]

It is by virtue of this devotion to an ideal, this concentration on a relationship, that love can become a power for self-transcendence. This is what Keats implies in his poem. The action leads up to a physical consummation; and, as Keats said in answer to criticism, this was inevitable. But in Keats's dialectical scheme nothing remains fixed within its own boundaries: everything, in so far as it achieves "intensity," is transmuted. And only at the point of maximum intensity can the possibility of transcendence be realized. This, in Donne's phrase, is love's alchemy. The idea is explicit in Keats's language:

> Beyond a mortal man impassion'd far
> At these voluptuous accents, he arose,
> Ethereal, flush'd, and like a throbbing star
> Seen mid the sapphire heaven's deep repose
> Into her dream he melted, as the rose
> Blendeth its odour with the violet,—

[5] Thus Keats will write to Fanny (13 October 1819): "—I could be martyr'd for my Religion—Love is my religion—I could die for that. . . ."

Solution sweet: meantime the frost-wind blows
Like Love's alarum pattering the sharp sleet
Against the window-panes; St. Agnes' moon hath set.

These lines—to my mind the supreme exemplar of "Romanticism" in English poetry—are precise in their statements. Porphyro is impassioned "beyond a mortal man"; he is "ethereal" (and we know by now what this means for Keats); he is like a star set in the deep repose of the unclouded sky (Keats's favourite eternity image). And he has attained this state, not through what Blake would call "negation," but through "energy" and "an improvement of sensual enjoyment." The stanza recognizes, moreover, life's bitter-sweet counterpoint: ". . . meantime the frost-wind blows."

I am afraid Benjamin Bailey was right when he accused Keats of approaching, in the second book of *Endymion,* "to that abominable principle of *Shelley's*—that *Sensual Love* is the principle of *things.*" [6] And Taylor, Keats's publisher, was right too about *The Eve of St. Agnes* when he wondered if "It was so natural a process in Keats's Mind to carry on the Train of his Story in the way he has done, that he could not write decently . . . if he had that Disease of the Mind which renders the Perceptions too dull to discover Right from Wrong in Matters of moral Taste." [7] For Keats, like Blake, was "a man without a mask." He could not pretend. As he saw, so he set down. He saw sensual love as a principle, and as such he presented it. What quite escaped Woodhouse and Bailey and Taylor was the bearing of Keats's other principle of *intensity*: the dialectical process.

In bringing *Endymion* and *St. Agnes' Eve* together like this I have suggested (what is indeed very obvious) the close connection between the two. Indeed, we can go farther. *Endymion,* which by any standards is Keats's major work (and as such I have treated it), contains in germ or in flower every single aspect of Keats's thinking and feeling and knowing. He put the whole of himself into it; and, what is more important, he put the whole of himself before disease and disappointment had conspired to warp, however slightly, that totality. *Endymion* is naïve, is immature, is garrulous; but it is

---

[6] Hyder Rollins, ed., *The Keats Circle,* I, 34.
[7] *K.C.,* I, 96.

unspoiled. If he had lived, Keats would doubtless have gone far
beyond it. But he did not live. He never wrote a poem of that
magnitude again. He tried, and gave up. *Endymion* remains, with
all its faults, Keats's most complete and most spontaneous expression of a total vision.

As such I have regarded it, and as such I shall continue to regard
it in this book. The significances of Keats's later poems reveal
themselves only when related to the total structure of *Endymion*.
Keats developed, of course; but he had not the time to develop
very far. The marvel is that, in so many respects, he had no need
to develop—only to consolidate and connect. The marvel is that
on so many points he was so unhesitatingly right.

Endymion is the great expansive, the great embracing poem. In
all that follows (with the partial exception of *Hyperion*) Keats
simply detaches and writes variations upon the themes of his
master-work. To put it in a slightly different way, the later poems
are focusing points for the great themes of *Endymion* which, now
from one angle and now from another, Keats examines and am-
plifies.

In *St. Agnes' Eve* Keats examines the thesis that love, human love,
is in itself a great good. When I say that he examines it I mean, of
course, that he examines it as a poet. He doesn't analyse it. He
doesn't rationalize the matter to himself. The word "examines" is
my rationalization, not his. He simply writes a poem because he
has to write a poem. But, viewed from *our* critical standpoint, that
is what *St. Agnes' Eve* is: a discussion of romantic love. The suggestion of *Endymion* that human love is "the chief intensity" is here
spot-lighted.[8] *Isabella* had shown the defeat of "vegetative" love.
St. Agnes' Eve shows the triumph of romantic love. Madeline and
Porphyro are in difficulties: but they do something about it. In the
midst of enemies they are undefeated: they go on, they achieve,
they escape. "O'er the southern moors" and they build a new life.

All this is implicit in the poem, and in the way Keats develops
the poem. That he develops it by contrasts is obvious enough.
What is less obvious, perhaps, is that the contrasts are based on a
life-death dichotomy, on a process from darkness (the root) to
light (the flower), and on the religious pattern of initiation. These

---

[8] The same principle is asserted in the "Bright Star" sonnet.

themes we have seen already treated in *Endymion*—indeed, in very great detail and complexity. Here they are isolated by Keats and confined to a local context.

My mention of initiation may seem pompous. But it is not unconsidered. The initiation ritual here in *St. Agnes' Eve* is as clear as in *Endymion*. Clearer perhaps, since the moment is isolated. Let us watch Porphyro's progress. Attracted by the adamant of Madeline's one-pointed concentration, he is drawn over the moors to the central castle. The castle is a place of peril (danger is an element in the initiation pattern). Evil forces are ready to assail him if he shrinks from the trial.

> For him, those chambers held barbarian hordes,
> Hyena foemen, and hot-blooded lords,
> Whose very dogs would execrations howl
> Against his lineage.

But Porphyro's heart is "on fire for Madeline." Her chamber is the central shrine to which he must win his way through whatever difficulties. And once he has achieved his initiation and gained the prize, all doors will open to him. Accompanied by his mystical bride, he has nothing to fear, in the event, from any Cerberus:

> The wakeful bloodhound rose, and shook his hide,
> But his sagacious eye an inmate owns:
> By one, and one, the bolts full easy slide.

The initiation begins with the lesser mysteries. Porphyro stands *outside* the castle, in darkness.

> Beside the portal doors,
> Buttress'd from moonlight, stands he, and implores
> All saints to give him sight of Madeline.

Then he ventures in. Still in accordance with the initiation pattern, he puts himself in the hands of a guide. Old Angela (the name is significant) first warns him of his danger: ". . . Porphyro! Hie thee from this place!" The warning is typical and constitutes the ritual putting-to-the-proof. But Porphyro is a true hero: he boldly accepts the challenge; and he is conducted on the third stage of his journey.

He follow'd through a lowly arched way,
Brushing the cobwebs with his lofty plume;
And as she mutter'd "Well-a—well-a-day!"
He found him in a little moonlight room,
Pale, latticed, chill, and silent as a tomb.

Threading the needle's eye, he finds himself in the place of waiting
where he must face a new trial—the testing of his faith and his
patience. He asks for a glimpse of Madeline. Angela continues to
express dismay at his daring:

"Thou must hold water in a witch's sieve,
And be liege-lord of all the Elves and Fays,
To venture so: it fills me with amaze
To see thee, Porphyro!"

Angela, admittedly, is a doddering old crone (she dies before the
night is out), but she is also a witch, a Sybil, a keeper of the mysteries:

Feebly she laugheth in the languid moon,
While Porphyro upon her face doth look,
Like puzzled urchin on an aged crone
Who keepeth clos'd a wond'rous riddle-book

With all his dash and courage, the hero is reduced to the condition
of a child, and it is the feeble old woman who holds the keys of his
success. She tells him now of "his lady's purpose" upon this Eve of
St. Agnes: of how Madeline too is seeking, is drawing her destiny
towards her by the power of enchantment.

And now, once again, the initiative is taken by the hero, while
the test is administered by the Sybil. He asks to be taken directly
to Madeline's chamber *in accordance with the prophecy* of which
he claims to be the fulfillment in person.[9] Angela charges him with
evil purposes, and commands him to go: but he remains firm, at-
testing his purity of intention: "I will not harm her, by all saints
I swear." Boldly he threatens to rouse the castle if his wish is
denied; and thus he forces the issue.

"Wait here, my child, with patience; kneel in prayer
The while . . . ,"

[9] The reference to Merlin and the "monstrous debt" paid to his "Demon" is
noteworthy (line 171).

Angela instructs him, before she goes off to prepare the ritual meal in Madeline's chamber. Porphyro is now exposed to the trial of patience: "The lover's endless minutes slowly pass'd." The old woman returns, and leads him on the fourth and last stage of his journey.

> Safe at last,
> Through many a dusky gallery, they gain
> The maiden's chamber, silken, hush'd, and chaste;
> Where Porphyro took covert, pleas'd amain.

If the vertical pattern of the poem is one of *growth* upward through successive levels of existence—mineral, vegetative, human, spiritual—the horizontal pattern is that of concentric circles of attainment to a central peace "at the heart Of endless agitation." The first or outer circle is that of the storm-lashed moor; the second circle is of the castle riotous with unholy feast and merriment; the third circle is Madeline's chamber. Here a concentration is achieved, under the moon's ægis, of the three worlds in the person of Madeline.

The moon reigns throughout *St. Agnes' Eve* as throughout *Endymion*. Her benign influence waxes with the progress of the action. While still outside the castle, Porphyro is "buttress'd from moonlight." This is the first mention of the moon. The second mention comes with the third stage of the journey: "He found him in a little moonlight room." The third mention comes with Madeline's entry into her chamber.

> Out went the taper as she hurried in;
> Its litle smoke, in pallid moonshine, died.
> She closed the door, she panted, all akin
> To spirits of the air, and visions wide.

The whole succeeding action of the poem is conducted in moonlight—within, that is to say, the circle of enchantment. Torchlight and candlelight, the impure flames of *this* world, must be extinguished. Only the moon-goddess now reigns. And it is she who concentres all her powers upon "the charmed maid" who is "like a mission'd spirit" for Porphyro's apotheosis. The focusing of light and power is through "a casement high and triple-arch'd," which

throws upon the kneeling girl the motley images of life: the life
of plants:

> Of fruits, and flowers, and bunches of knot-grass;

the life of minerals:

> And diamonded with panes of quaint device,
> Innumerable of stains and splendid dyes;

the life of animals:

> . . . the tiger-moth's deep-damask'd wings;

and of men:

> . . . in the midst, 'mong thousand heraldries,
>   And twilight saints, and dim emblazonings,
> A shielded scutcheon blush'd with blood of queens and kings.

Madeline kneels at the centre of all this glory. Note that the
cross, Keats's great reconciling symbol, is the inner focus which
redirects, with its silver shining, a ray of the glory to Porphyro's
eyes.

> Full on this casement shone the wintry moon,
> And threw warm gules on Madeline's fair breast,
> As down she knelt for heaven's grace and boon;
> Rose-bloom fell on her hands, together prest,
> And on her silver cross soft amethyst,
> And on her hair a glory, like a saint:
> She seem'd a splendid angel, newly drest,
> Save wings, for heaven:—Porphyro grew faint:
> She knelt, so pure a thing, so free from mortal taint.

At this point the vigorous and decisive action of the poem (contrasting so powerfully with the languor of *Isabella* and the mean-
derings of *Endymion*) is immobilized, like a stream suddenly frozen
under a "wintry moon." There is a moment of absolute stillness.
All human warmth and passion are withdrawn. But the moment
cannot continue. Warmth and passion must return: for the action
is working up to a climax not of abnegation, but of identification
and fruition. The human and the spiritual loves must, as in *Endymion*, be reconciled.

The next two stanzas, therefore, offer us a cluster of highly sensual images, as Madeline "unclasps her warmed jewels one by one, loosens her fragrant bodice," and lies down in her soft nest "until the poppied warmth of sleep" finally overcomes her. The contrast with the previous stanza is powerful, but not incongruous. Similarly, we have the silence of the bedchamber suddenly broken, but not permanently, by

> The boisterous, midnight, festive clarion,
> The kettle-drum, and far-head clarionet

as the hall-door below opens for a moment and shuts again.

Now comes the setting-out of the ritual meal. This central feature of the initiation pattern is developed with all Keats's mastery of tactile, non-visual sensory detail. The visual has been given us already in the triple-arched casement: now we must grasp the sacramental through the media of taste and smell and touch. Upon the altar-table, with its cloth "of woven crimson, gold and jet," the non-animal, initiatory food [10] is set out in presence of the sleeping maid:

> And still she slept an azure-lidded sleep,
> In blanched linen, smooth, and lavender'd,
> While he from forth the closet brought a heap
> Of candied apple, quince, and plum, and gourd
> With jellies soother than the creamy curd,
> And lucent syrops, tinct with cinnamon;
> Manna and dates, in argosy transferr'd
> From Fez; and spiced dainties, every one,
> From silken Samarcand to cedar'd Lebanon.

And here once again we have, transposed into the key of food, of the sacramental meal, the same idea of the concentration of Nature's store: "infinite riches in a little room."

Porphyro wakes Madeline to share the sacrament. He wakes her with music—the "ancient ditty" of "La belle dame sans mercy." Her dream extends—after a last trial of doubt and fear for Porphyro and herself—into the waking bliss of consummation. So the fourth circle, of physical passion which by its supreme "intensity"

[10] A cancelled item of the window's store—"sunny corn ears parched"—recalls the final revelation to the initiate in the Eleusinian mysteries.

is spiritual and spiritualizes, is attained: "St Agnes' moon hath set."

> "Ah, silver shrine, here will I take my rest
> After so many hours of toil and quest,
> A famish'd pilgrim,—saved by miracle."

But the pattern of initiation is conflated—as so often—with the pattern of deliverance: Persephone is not only the goddess, the final revelation of the mysteries, she is also the Kore, the imprisoned maiden who must be rescued and restored to freedom by Hermes. The story is identical in this respect with that of Orpheus and Eurydice: and Madeline's caution in embarking on her "dream" underlines this point:

> [She] dares not look behind, or all the charm is fled.

So, with the escape past "sleeping dragons," "wakeful bloodhound," and armed foes, the story ends. It is a love story, as purely sensuous and passionate as *The Song of Solomon,* and as much an allegory of spiritual awakening; it is an adventure story, as brisk and straightforward as any tale of the Round Table, and as complete an expression of the age-old pattern of initiation and achievement. It is set firmly in the Gothic north of castles, storms, hermits and witches, but its meaning constantly spills over into the wider and sunnier currents of Keats's beloved Greece.

The Hoodwinking of Madeline:
Skepticism in "The Eve of St. Agnes"

by Jack Stillinger

I

The commonest response to *The Eve of St. Agnes* has been the celebration of its "heady and perfumed loveliness." The poem has been called "a monody of dreamy richness," "one long sensuous utterance," "an expression of lyrical emotion," "a great affirmation of love," "a great choral hymn," an expression of "unquestioning rapture," and many things else. Remarks like these tend to confirm one's uneasy feeling that what is sometimes called "the most perfect" of Keats's longer poems is a mere fairy-tale romance, unhappily short on meaning. For many readers, as for Douglas Bush, the poem is "no more than a romantic tapestry of unique richness of color"; one is "moved less by the experience of the characters than . . . by the incidental and innumerable beauties of descriptive phrase and rhythm." [1]

To be sure, not all critics have merely praised Keats's pictures.

"The Hoodwinking of Madeline: Scepticism in The Eve of St. Agnes*" by Jack Stillinger. From* Studies in Philology *58 (1961). Reprinted by permission of the author and the University of North Carolina Press.*

[1] John Keats, *Selected Poems and Letters* (Boston, 1959), pp. xvi, 333; see also Bush's "Keats and His Ideas," in *The Major English Romantic Poets: A Symposium in Reappraisal*, ed. Clarence D. Thorpe, et al. (Carbondale, Ill., 1957), pp. 239f. The view is sanctioned by Keats himself, who thought the poem was in some ways like "Isabella"—"too smokeable," with "too much inexperience of . . . [life], and simplicity of knowledge in it," "A weak-sided Poem"; when he later planned a new attempt in poetry, it was "the colouring of St. Agnes eve" that he would "diffuse . . . throughout a Poem in which Character and Sentiment would be the figures to such drapery" (*The Letters of John Keats*, ed. Hyder E. Rollins, Cambridge, Mass., 1958, II, 174, 234).

After all, the poem opens on a note of "bitter chill," and progresses through images of cold and death before the action gets under way. When young Porphyro comes from across the moors to claim his bride, he enters a hostile castle, where Madeline's kinsmen will murder even upon holy days; and in the face of this danger he proceeds to Madeline's bedchamber. With the sexual consummation of their love, a storm comes up, and they must escape the castle, past "sleeping dragons," porter, and bloodhound, out into the night. The ending reverts to the opening notes of bitter chill and death: Madeline's kinsmen are benightmared, the old Beadsman and Madeline's nurse Angela are grotesquely dispatched into the next world. Some obvious contrasts are made in the poem: the lovers' youth and vitality are set against the old age and death associated with Angela and the Beadsman; the warmth and security of Madeline's chamber are contrasted with the coldness and hostility of the rest of the castle and the icy storm outside; the innocence and purity of young love are played off against the sensuousness of the revellers elsewhere in the castle; and so on. Through these contrasts, says one critic, Keats created a tale of young love "not by forgetting what everyday existence is like, but by using the mean, sordid, and commonplace as a foundation upon which to build a high romance"; the result is no mere fairy tale, but a poem that "has a rounded fulness, a complexity and seriousness, a balance which remove it from the realm of mere magnificent tour de force." [2]

But still something is wanting. The realistic notes all seem to occur in the framework, and the main action is all romance. There is no interaction between the contrasting elements, and hence no conflict. Porphyro is never really felt to be in danger; through much of the poem the lovers are secluded from the rest of the world; and at the end, when they escape, they meet no obstacle, but rather "glide, like phantoms, into the wide hall; / Like phantoms, to the iron porch, they glide. . . . By one, and one, the bolts full easy slide:— / The chains lie silent . . . The key turns . . . the door upon its hinges groans. / And they are gone" (361–370). It is all too easy. Though the poem ends with the nightmares of the

[2] R. H. Fogle, "A Reading of Keats's 'Eve of St. Agnes,'" *CE*, VI (1945), 328, 325.

warriors, and the deaths of Angela and the Beadsman, the lovers seem untouched, for they have already fled the castle. And besides, this all happened "ages long ago" (370). We are back where we started, with a fairy-tale romance, unhappily short on meaning.

The only serious attempt to make something of the poem has come from a small group of critics whom I shall call "metaphysical critics" because they think Keats was a metaphysician. To them the poem seems to dramatize certain ideas that Keats held a year or two earlier about the nature of the imagination, the relationship between this world and the next, and the progress of an individual's ascent toward spiritualization.

According to the popular superstition connected with St. Agnes' Eve, a young maiden who fasts and neither speaks nor looks about before she goes to bed may get sight of her future husband in a dream. Madeline follows this prescription, dreams of her lover, then seems to awaken out of her dream to find him present in her chamber, an actual, physical fact. Her dream in a sense comes true. The events are thought to relate to a passage in the well-known letter to Benjamin Bailey, 22 November 1817, in which Keats expressed his faith in "the truth of Imagination": "What the imagination seizes as Beauty must be truth—whether it existed before or not. . . . The Imagination may be compared to Adam's dream —he awoke and found it truth." For the metaphysical critics, just as Adam dreamed of the creation of Eve, then awoke to find his dream a truth—Eve before him a beautiful reality—so Madeline dreams of Porphyro and awakens to find him present and palpably real.

But the imagination is not merely prophetic: it is "a Shadow of reality to come" hereafter; and in the same letter Keats is led on to "another favorite Speculation"—"that we shall enjoy ourselves hereafter by having what we called happiness on Earth repeated in a finer tone and so repeated. . . . Adam's dream will do here and seems to be a conviction that Imagination and its empyreal reflection is the same as human Life and its spiritual repetition." The idea is that a trust in the visionary imagination will allow us to "burst our mortal bars," to "dodge / Conception to the very bourne of heaven," to transcend our earthly confines, guess at heaven, and arrive at some view of the reality to come. If the visionary imagination is valid, the earthly pleasures portrayed in our visions will make up our immortal existence—will be spiritually "repeated in a finer tone and so repeated."

In this sense, Madeline's dream of Porphyro is a case history in the visionary imagination. According to the metaphysical critics, she is, in her dream, at heaven's bourne, already enjoying a kind of spiritual repetition of earthly happiness. On being roused by Porphyro, she finds in him "a painful change" (300): "How chang'd thou art! how pallid, chill, and drear!" she says to him; "Give me that voice again . . . Those looks immortal" (311–313). Porphyro's reply takes the form of action: "Beyond a mortal man impassion'd far / At these voluptuous accents, he arose" (316f.). He transcends his mortal existence, joins Madeline at heaven's bourne by melting into her dream, and together they store up pleasures to be immortally repeated in a finer tone.

The other main strand of the critics' thinking concerns the apotheosis of Porphyro. By relating the poem to Keats's simile of human life as a "Mansion of Many Apartments," the critics would persuade us that the castle of Madeline's kinsmen allegorically represents human life, and that Porphyro, passing upward to a closet adjoining Madeline's bedchamber, and thence into the chamber itself, progresses from apartment to apartment in the mansion of life, executing a spiritual ascent to heaven's bourne. For a number of reasons, Keats's simile confuses rather than clarifies the poem.[3] But the idea of spiritual pilgrimage is not entirely to be denied. Porphyro says to the sleeping Madeline, "Thou art my heaven, and I thine eremite" (277), and when she awakens, after the consummation, he exclaims to her: "Ah, silver shrine, here will I take my rest / After so many hours of toil and quest, / A famish'd pilgrim,—saved by miracle" (337–339).

In brief summary, the main points of the metaphysical critics'

---

[3] The simile occurs in a letter to J. H. Reynolds, 3 May 1818 (*Letters*, I, 280f.). Porphyro's eagerness to get to Madeline hardly accords with Keats's idea that "we care not to hasten" to "the second Chamber"; the identification of Madeline's bedroom with "the Chamber of Maiden-Thought" seems similarly unfitting, since one of the effects of arriving in the latter is "that tremendous one of sharpening ones vision into the heart and nature of Man—of convincing one's nerves that the World is full of Misery and Heartbreak, Pain, Sickness and oppression."

interpretation are that Madeline's awakening to find Porphyro in her bedroom is a document in the validity of the visionary imagination; that Porphyro in the course of the poem makes a spiritual pilgrimage, ascending higher by stages until he arrives at transcendent reality in Madeline's bed; and that there the lovers reenact earthly pleasures that will be stored up for further, still more elevated repetition in a finer tone. If these ideas seem farfetched and confused, the fact should be attributed in part to the brevity of my exposition, and to the shortcomings of any attempt to abstract ideas from a complicated poem, even when it is treated as allegory. Yet one may suggest reasons for hesitating to accept them.

For one thing, when the imaginative vision of beauty turns out to be a truth—when Madeline awakens to find Porphyro in her bed—she is not nearly so pleased as Adam was when he awoke and discovered Eve. In fact, truth here is seemingly undesirable: Madeline is frightened out of her wits, and she laments, "No dream, alas! alas! and woe is mine! / Porphyro will leave me here to fade and pine" (328f.). For another, it is a reversal of Keats's own sequence to find in the poem the spiritual repetition of earthly pleasures. In Madeline's dream the imaginative enactment of pleasure comes first; it is an earthly repetition of spiritual pleasure that follows, and perhaps in a grosser, rather than a finer, tone. That the lovers are consciously intent on experiencing the conditions of immortality—consciously practising for the spiritual repetition of pleasure at an even higher level of intensity—implies, if one reads the critics correctly, that both Madeline and Porphyro have read *Endymion,* Keats's letters, and the explications of the metaphysical critics.

Much of the critics' interpretation rests on the religious language of the poem. Madeline is "St. Agnes' charmed maid," "a mission'd spirit" (192f.), "all akin / To spirits of the air" (201f.), "a saint," "a splendid angel, newly drest, / Save wings, for heaven," "so pure a thing, so free from mortal taint" (222–225). To Porphyro, her "eremite," she is "heaven" (277), and from closet to bedchamber he progresses from purgatory to paradise. Finally, Porphyro is "A famish'd pilgrim,—saved by miracle" (339). But the significance of such language is questionable. In *Romeo and Juliet,* with which *The Eve of St. Agnes* has much in common, Juliet's hand at the first meeting of the lovers is a "holy shrine," and Romeo's lips are "two blushing pilgrims"; subsequently Juliet is a "dear saint," a "bright angel," a "fair saint"; "heaven is . . . Where Juliet lives," and outside Verona is "purgatory, torture, hell itself"; she is compared to a "winged messenger of heaven," and her lips carry "immortal blessing." At the same time Romeo is "the god of . . . [Juliet's] idolatry," and a "mortal paradise of . . . sweet flesh." [4] In other poems Keats himself, in the manner of hundreds of poets before him, uses religious terms in hyperbolic love language: for example, Isabella's lover Lorenzo is called "a young palmer in Love's eye," he is said to "shrive" his passion, and (in a stanza ultimately rejected from the poem) he declares that he would be "full deified" by the gift of a love token.[5]

What is perhaps most telling against the critics, in connection with the religious language of *The Eve of St. Agnes,* is that when Porphyro calls himself "A famish'd pilgrim,—saved by miracle," his words must be taken ironically, unless Keats has forgotten, or hopes the reader has forgotten, all the action leading to the consummation. The miracle on which Porphyro congratulates himself is in fact a *stratagem* that he has planned and carried out to perfection. Early in the poem, when he first encounters Angela, she is amazed to see him, and says that he "must hold water in a witch's sieve, / And be liege-lord of all the Elves and Fays, / To venture" into a castle of enemies (120–122). Although Porphyro later assures Madeline that he is "no rude infidel" (342), the images in Angela's speech tend to link him with witches and fairies rather than with the Christian pilgrim. By taking a closer look at the poem, we may see that Keats had misgivings about Porphyro's fitness to perform a spiritual pilgrimage and arrive at heaven.

II

Porphyro's first request of Angela, "Now tell me where is Madeline" (114), is followed by an oath upon the holy loom used to

---

[4] I. v. 96f., 105; II. ii. 26, 55, 61; III. iii. 29f., 18; II. ii. 28; III. iii 37; II. ii. 114; III. ii. 82.

[5] Lines 2, 64, and the rejected stanza following line 56 (*The Poetical Works of John Keats,* ed. H. W. Garrod, 2nd edn., Oxford, 1958, p. 217n.).

weave St. Agnes' wool, and it is implied that he is well aware what night it is. "St. Agnes' Eve," says Angela, "God's help! my lady fair the conjuror plays / This very night: gold angels her deceive!" (123–125). While she laughs at Madeline's folly, Porphyro gazes on her, until "Sudden a thought came like a full-blown rose. . . . then doth he propose / A stratagem" (136–139). The full force of "stratagem" comes to be felt in the poem—a ruse, an artifice, a trick for deceiving. For Angela, the deception of Madeline by good angels is funny; but Porphyro's is another kind of deception, and no laughing matter. She is startled, and calls him "cruel," "impious," "wicked" (140, 143); the harshness of the last line of her speech emphasizes her reaction: "Thou canst not surely be the same that thou didst seem" (144).

Porphyro swears "by all saints" not to harm Madeline: "O may I ne'er find grace / When my weak voice shall whisper its last prayer, / If one of her soft ringlets I displace" (145–148). He next enforces his promise with a suicidal threat: Angela must believe him, or he "will . . . Awake, with horrid shout" his foemen, "And beard them" (151–153). Because Angela is "A poor, weak, palsy-stricken, churchyard thing" (155), she presently accedes, promising to do whatever Porphyro wishes—

> Which was, to lead him, in close secrecy,
> Even to Madeline's chamber, and there hide
> Him in a closet, of such privacy
> That he might see her beauty unespied,
> And win perhaps that night a peerless bride,
> While legion'd fairies pac'd the coverlet,
> And pale enchantment held her sleepy-eyed. (163–169)

At this point our disbelief must be suspended if we are to read the poem as an affirmation of romantic love. We must leave our world behind, where stratagems like Porphyro's are frowned on, sometimes punished in the criminal courts, and enter an imaginary world where "in sooth such things have been" (81). But the narrator's summary comment on the stratagem is that "Never on such a night have lovers met, / Since Merlin paid his Demon all the monstrous debt" (170f.). The allusion is puzzling. Commentators feel that the "monstrous debt" is Merlin's debt to his demon-father for his own life, and that he paid it by committing evil deeds, or perhaps specifically by effecting his own imprisonment and death through the misworking of a spell. However it is explained, it strengthens rather than dispels our suspicion, like Angela's, that Porphyro is up to no good; and, with the earlier images of "legion'd fairies" and "pale enchantment," it brings further associations of fairy-lore and sorcery to bear on his actions. Then Angela asserts a kind of orthodox middle-class morality: "Ah! thou must needs the lady wed" (179).

She now leads Porphyro to Madeline's chamber, "silken, hush'd, and chaste," where he takes "covert'" (187f.). In the first draft Stanza XXI is incomplete, but two versions that can be pieced together call Porphyro's hiding-place "A purgatory sweet to view love's own domain" and "A purgatory sweet to what may he attain." The rejected lines, mentioning "purgatory sweet" as a stage toward the "paradise" (244) of Madeline's chamber, are documents in Porphyro's spiritual pilgrimage, perhaps. The ideas of viewing love's own domain, or what he may attain, are documents in the peeping-Tomism that occupies the next few stanzas. As Angela is feeling her way toward the stair, she is met by Madeline, who turns back to help her down to "a safe level matting" (196). If the action is significant, its meaning lies in the juxtaposition of Madeline's unselfish act of "pious care" (194) with the leering overtones just before of Porphyro's having hidden himself in her closet, "pleas'd amain" (188)—pleased exceedingly by the success of his stratagem—and with the tone of the narrator's words immediately following: "Now prepare, / Young Porphyro, for gazing on that bed; / She comes, she comes again, like ring-dove fray'd and fled" (196–198).

The mention of "ring-dove" is interesting. Porphyro has taken "covert"—the position of the hunter (or perhaps merely the bird-watcher). There follows a series of bird images that perhaps may be thought of in terms of the hunter's game. In a variant to the stanza Madeline is "an affrighted Swan"; here she is a "ring-dove"; in the next stanza her heart is "a tongueless nightingale" (206); later in the poem she is "A dove forlorn" (333); still later Porphyro speaks or robbing her nest (340), and in a variant says, "Soft Nightingale, I'll keep thee in a cage / To sing to me." [6] It is unlikely that all

[6] For the variants see Garrod, pp. 245n., 253n.

these images carry connotations of hunting, nest-robbing, and caging; Romeo will "climb a bird's nest" when he ascends the ladder to Juliet's room (II. v. 76). But the single comparison of Madeline's heart to a "tongueless nightingale" seems significant. Leigh Hunt naturally missed the point: "The nightingale! how touching the simile! the heart a 'tongueless nightingale,' dying in that dell of the bosom. What thorough sweetness, and perfection of lovely imagery!" Critics pointing to Sotheby's translation of Wieland's *Oberon* (VI. 17), or to *Troilus and Criseyde* (III. 1233–39),[7] may also have missed the significance. For Keats's image embraces the entire story of the rape of Philomel, and with it he introduces a further note of evil that prevents us from losing ouselves in the special morality of fairy romance. Madeline has the status of one of St. Agnes' "lambs unshorn" (71); she is a maiden innocent and pure, but also is about to lose that status through what is in some ways a cruel deception. The comparison with Philomel is not inappropriate.

In Stanza XXV, as Madeline is described kneeling, we are told that "Porphyro grew faint: / She knelt, so pure a thing, so free from mortal taint" (224f.). Though many reasons will suggest themselves why Porphyro grows faint, a novel one may be offered here. In his copy of *The Anatomy of Melancholy*, after a passage in which Burton tells how "The Barbarians stand in awe of a fair woman, and at a beautiful aspect, a fierce spirit is pacified," Keats wrote, "abash'd the devil stood." He quotes from Book IV of *Paradise Lost*, where Satan is confronted by the beautiful angel Zephon: "Abasht the Devil stood, / And felt how awful goodness is, and saw / Virtue in her shape how lovely, saw, and pin'd / His loss" (846–849). But since Burton speaks of standing "in awe of a fair woman" Keats must also have recalled Book IX, in which Satan's malice is momentarily overawed by Eve's graceful innocence: "That space the Evil one abstracted stood / From his own evil, and for the time remain'd / Stupidly good" (463–465). Porphyro's faintness may in some way parallel Satan's moment of stupid goodness. "But the hot Hell that always in him burns" soon ends Satan's

[7] *Leigh Hunt's London Journal*, II (1835), 18; Sidney Colvin, *John Keats* (New York, 1925), p. 87n.; F. E. L. Priesteley, "Keats and Chaucer," *MLQ*, V (1944), 444.

relapse from evil intent, as he goes about Eve's ruin. So with Porphyro; for "Anon his heart revives" (226), as he pursues the working-out of his stratagem.

Madeline undresses, then falls fast asleep. Porphyro creeps to the
bed, "Noiseless as fear in a wide wilderness" (250), and "'tween
the curtains peep'd, where, lo!—how fast she slept" (252). At the
bedside he sets a table, when, in the midst of his preparations, a
hall-door opens in the castle, and the revellers' music shatters the
silence of the room. Porphyro calls for a "drowsy Morphean amulet" (257)—and then "The hall door shuts . . . and all the noise
is gone" (261). Madeline continues sleeping, while he brings from
the closet the feast of candied apple, quince, plum, and all the
rest.

Aside from the unheroic implications of "Noiseless as fear in a
wide wilderness" and of the word "peep'd," there are three things
worth noting in the stanzas just summarized. One is the relationship the poem has at this point with *Cymbeline*, II. ii. 11–50, in
which the villainous Iachimo emerges from the trunk, where he
has hidden himself, to gaze on the sleeping Imogen. Readers since
Swinburne have noted resemblances. Imogen is "a heavenly angel,"
and like Madeline a "fresh lily," "whiter than the sheets," as she
lies in bed, sleeping, in effect, an "azure-lidded sleep" (262)—and
so on. But no critic has been willing to include among the resemblances that Porphyro's counterpart in the scene is a villain. In
the speech from which these details have been drawn, Iachimo com-
pares himself with Tarquin, who raped Lucrece, and he notes that
Imogen "hath been reading late / The tale of Tereus; here the
leaf's turn'd down / Where Philomel gave up."

The second point concerns Porphyro's call for a "drowsy Morphean amulet"—a sleep-inducing charm to prevent Madeline's
awakening when the music bursts forth into the room. Earlier he
has wished to win Madeline while "pale enchantment held her
sleepy-eyed" (169). Here he would assist "pale enchantment" with
a "Morphean amulet." It may not be amiss to recall Lovelace, and
the stratagem by which he robbed Clarissa of her maidenhood. "I
know thou wilt blame me for having had recourse to *Art*," writes
Lovelace to John Belford, in Richardson's novel. "But do not phy-

sicians prescribe opiates in acute cases." Besides, "a Rape, thou
knowest, to us Rakes, is far from being an undesirable thing." [8]

The third point concerns the feast that Porphyro sets out. In
his copy of *The Anatomy of Melancholy,* opposite a passage in
which Burton commends fasting as an excellent means of preparation for devotion, "by which chast thoughts are ingendred . . .
concupiscence is restrained, vicious . . . lusts and humours are ex-
pelled," Keats recorded his approval in the marginal comment
"good." It is for some reason of this sort that Madeline fasts, going
"supperless to bed" (51). Porphyro's feast seems intended to produce the opposite results, and there is more than a suggestion of
pagan sensuality in the strange affair of eastern luxuries that he
heaps as if by magic—"with glowing hand" (271)—on the table by
the bed.

Next Porphyro tries to awaken Madeline, or so it seems: "And
now, my love, my seraph fair, awake! / Thou art my heaven, and
I thine eremite" (276f.). The last line carries the suggestion that
Porphyro has been reading of the martyrdom, not of St. Agnes,
but of Donne's lovers in "The Canonization," whose bodies are by
"reverend love" made "one another's hermitage." It is curious that
in the proposition that follows, "Open thine eyes . . . Or I shall
drowse beside thee" (278f.), Porphyro does not wait for an answer:
"Thus whispering, his warm, unnerved arm / Sank in her pillow"
(280f.). "Awakening up" (289), he takes Madeline's lute and plays
an ancient ditty, which causes her to utter a soft moan. It would
seem that she does at this point wake up: "Suddenly / Her blue
affrayed eyes wide open shone. . . . Her eyes were open, but she
still beheld, / Now wide awake, the vision of her sleep" (295–299).
Not unreasonably, we might think, she weeps, sighs, and "moan[s]
forth witless words" (303).

We shall see in a moment, however, that she has not after all
awakened from her trance. The "painful change" she witnesses—
the substitution of the genuine Porphyro for the immortal looks
and voice of her vision—*"nigh* expell'd / The blisses of her dream"
(300f.), came near expelling them, but did not in fact do so. Apparently she is to be thought of as still in her trance, but capable

[8] *Clarissa,* Shakespeare Head edn. (Oxford, 1930), V, 339f.

of speaking to the Porphyro before her, when she says, "Ah, Porphyro! . . . but even now / Thy voice was at sweet tremble in mine ear" (307f.). To her request for "that voice again . . . Those looks immortal" (312f.), Porphyro offers neither, but rather impassioned action of godlike intensity. At the end of Stanza XXXVI, the image of "St. Agnes' moon" combines the notions of St. Agnes, the patron saint of maidenhood, and Cynthia, the goddess of chastity, and the symbolic combination has "set," gone out of the picture to be replaced by a storm: "Meantime the frost-wind blows / Like Love's alarum pattering the sharp sleet / Against the window-panes; St. Agnes' moon hath set" (322–324).

Keats's final manuscript version of the consummation, rejected by his publishers on moral grounds, as making the poem unfit to be read by young ladies, is more graphic. For a rather lame conclusion to Madeline's speech (314f.), he substituted the lines, "See while she speaks his arms encroaching slow / Have zon'd her, heart to heart—loud, loud the dark winds blow." Then he rewrote Stanza XXXVI:

> For on the midnight came a tempest fell.
> More sooth for that his close rejoinder flows
> Into her burning ear;—and still the spell
> Unbroken guards her in serene repose.
> With her wild dream he mingled as a rose
> Marryeth its odour to a violet.
> Still, still she dreams—louder the frost wind blows
> Like Love's alarum pattering the sharp sleet
> Against the window-panes; St. Agnes' moon hath set.[9]

The revised version makes clearer that Madeline is still dreaming: "still the spell / Unbroken guards her in serene repose." And it

[9] Garrod, p. 252n. After hearing the revised version, Richard Woodhouse wrote to the publisher John Taylor, 19 September 1819, "I do apprehend it will render the poem unfit for ladies, & indeed scarcely to be mentioned to them among the 'things that are.'" Taylor replied six days later that if Keats "will not so far concede to my Wishes as to leave the passage as it originally stood, I must be content to admire his Poems with some other Imprint" (*Letters,* II, 163, 183). According to Woodhouse's note heading one of the transcripts of the poem, Keats "left it to his Publishers to adopt which [alterations] they pleased, & to revise the whole" (Garrod, p. xxxviii). Though the argument cannot be made here, there are grounds for urging that a new text be made, embodying re-

makes clearer the connection between the sexual consummation, the setting of St. Agnes' moon, and the rising of the storm. When Porphyro's "close rejoinder flows / Into . . . [the] burning ear" of Madeline, we may or may not recall Satan "Squat like a Toad, close at the ear of *Eve*" (IV. 800); but one would go out of his way to avoid a parallel between the advent of the storm in Keats's poem and the change in Nature that comes about when our first mother in an evil hour reached forth and ate the fruit: "Earth felt the wound, and Nature from her seat / Sighing through all her Works gave signs of woe, / That all was lost" (IX. 782–784). Unlike Eve, however, rather more like Clarissa, Madeline by this time has no choice; the revision heightens the contrast between her innocent unconsciousness and the storm raging outside: "Still, still she dreams—louder the frost wind blows."

As printed, the poem continues: " 'Tis dark: quick pattereth the flaw-blown sleet." Then Porphyro: "This is no dream, my bride, my Madeline!" Another line describes the storm: " 'Tis dark: the iced gusts still rave and beat" (325–327). And now Madeline finally does wake up, if she ever does. Her speech shows a mixed attitude toward what has happened, but above all it is the lament of the seduced maiden: "No dream, alas! alas! and woe is mine! / Porphyro will leave me here to fade and pine.— / Cruel! what traitor could thee hither bring?" (328–330). She will curse not, for her heart is lost in his, or, perhaps more accurately, still lost in her romantic idealization of him. But she is aware that her condition is woeful: Porphyro is cruel; Angela is a traitor; and Madeline is a "deceived thing;— / A dove forlorn and lost" (333). In subsequent stanzas Porphyro soothes her fears, again calls her his bride, and seems to make all wrongs right. He tells her that the storm outside is really only "an elfin-storm from faery land" (343), and that she should "Awake! arise! . . . and fearless be, / For o'er the southern moors I have a home for thee" (350f.). They hurry out of the chamber, down the wide stairs, through the castle door— "And they are gone . . . fled away into the storm" (370f.).

III

After giving so much space to Porphyro, in admittedly exaggerated fashion portraying him as peeping Tom and villainous seducer, I must now confess that I do not think his stratagem is the main concern of the poem. I have presented him as villain in order to suggest, in the first place, that he is not, after all, making a spiritual pilgrimage, unless the poem is to be read as a satire on spiritual pilgrimages; in the second place, that the lovers, far from being a single element in the poem, are as much protagonist and antagonist as Belinda and the Baron, or Clarissa and Lovelace; and in the third place, that no matter how much Keats entered into the feelings of his characters, he could not lose touch with the claims and responsibilities of the world he lived in.

Certainly he partially identified himself with Porphyro. When Woodhouse found his revisions objectionable, Keats replied that he should "despise a man who would be such an eunuch in sentiment as to leave a maid, with that Character about her, in such a situation: & sho^d despise himself to write about it." One may cite the narrator's obvious relish in Porphyro's situation as Madeline is about to undress—"Now prepare, / Young Porphyro, for gazing on that bed" (196f.)—and Keats's later objection to the poem that "in my dramatic capacity I enter fully into the feeling: but in Propria Persona I should be apt to quiz it myself." But sexual passion worried him: to Bailey he confessed in July 1818, "When I am among Women I have evil thoughts," and he wrote in his copy of *The Anatomy of Melancholy,* "there is nothing disgraces me in my own eyes so much as being one of a race of eyes nose and mouth beings in a planet call'd the earth who . . . have always mingled goatish winnyish lustful love with the abstract adoration of the deity." Though it has touches of humor, *The Eve of St. Agnes* is a serious poem; regardless of the extent to which Keats identified with his hero, he introduced enough overtones of evil to make Porphyro's actions wrong within the structure of the poem.

From now on, however, it may be best to think of Porphyro as representing, like the storm that comes up simultaneously with his conquest, the ordinary cruelties of life in the world. Like Melville, Keats saw

> Too for into the sea; where every man.
> The greater on the less feeds evermore. . . .
> Still do I that most fierce destruction see,
> The Shark at savage prey—the hawk at pounce,
> The gentle Robin, like a pard or ounce,
> Ravening a worm.[10]

Let Porphyro represent one of the sharks under the surface. And to borrow another figure from Melville, let the main concern of the poem be the young Platonist dreaming at the masthead: one false step, his identity comes back in horror, and with a half-throttled shriek he drops through transparent air into the sea, no more to rise for ever. There are reasons why we ought not entirely to sympathize with Madeline. She is a victim of deception, to be sure, but of deception not so much by Porphyro as by herself and the superstition she trusts in. Madeline the self-hoodwinked dreamer is, I think, the main concern of the poem, and I shall spend some time documenting this notion and relating it to Keat's other important poems—all of which, in a sense, are about dreaming.

If we recall Keats's agnosticism, his sonnet "Written in Disgust of Vulgar Superstition" (Christianity), and his abuse in the *Letters* of "the pious frauds of Religion," we may be prepared to see a hoodwinked dreamer in the poem even before we meet Madeline. He is the old Beadsman, so engrossed in an ascetic ritual that he is sealed off from the joys of life. After saying his prayers, he turns first through a door leading to the noisy revelry upstairs. "But no. . . . The joys of all his life were said and sung: / His was a harsh penance on St. Agnes' Eve" (22–24). And so he goes another way, to sit among rough ashes, while the focus of the narrative proceeds through the door he first opened, and on into the assembly of revellers, where we are introduced to Madeline and the ritual she is intent on following. In the final manuscript version, between Stanzas VI and VII, Keats inserted an additional stanza on the ritual, in part to explain the feast that Porphyro sets out:

[10] "To J. H. Reynolds, Esq.," ll. 93–95, 102–105 (Garrod, p. 487).

'Twas said her future lord would there appear
Offering as sacrifice—all in the dream—
Delicious food even to her lips brought near:
Viands and wine and fruit and sugar'd cream,
To touch her palate with the fine extreme
Of relish: then soft music heard; and then
More pleasure followed in a dizzy stream
Palpable almost: then to wake again
Warm in the virgin morn, no weeping Magdalen.[11]

Then the poem, as it was printed, continues describing Madeline, who scarcely hears the music, and, with eyes fixed on the floor, pays no attention to anyone around her.

Several things deserve notice. By brooding "all that wintry day, / On love, and wing'd St. Agnes' saintly care" (43f.), and by setting herself apart from the revellers, Madeline presents an obvious parallel with the Beadsman. Both are concerned with prayer and an ascetic ritual; both are isolated from the crowd and from actuality. A second point is that the superstition is clearly an old wives' tale: Madeline follows the prescription that "she had heard old dames full many times declare" (45). It is called by the narrator a "whim": "Full of this whim was thoughtful Madeline" (55). The irony of the added stanza enforces the point. Madeline's pleasures turn out to be palpable in fact. When she awakens to find herself with Porphyro, she is anything but warm: rather, she wakes up to "flaw-blown sleet" and "iced gusts" (325, 327); it is no virgin morn for her; and she is a "weeping Magdalen," who cries, "alas! alas! and woe is mine!" (328). But at this point, early in the poem, "she saw not: her heart was otherwise: / She sigh'd for Agnes' dreams, the sweetest of the year" (62f.). Perfunctorily dancing along, she is said to be "Hoodwink'd with faery fancy; all amort, / Save to St. Agnes and her lambs unshorn" (70f.).

The superstition is next mentioned when Angela tells that Madeline "the conjuror plays / This very night: good angels her deceive!" (124f.). Porphyro thinks of the ritual in terms of "enchantments cold" and "legends old" (134f.). Proceeding to her chamber,

---

[11] Garrod, p. 238n. In Ben Jonson's quatrain, quoted by Hunt from Brand's *Popular Antiquities* and often cited in notes to Keats's poem, the assurance that the ritual produces "an *empty* dream" is worth recalling (*Leigh Hunt's London Journal*, II, 1835, 17).

Madeline is called "St. Agnes' charmed maid," "a mission'd spirit, unaware" (192f.). When she undresses, "Half-hidden, like a mermaid in sea-weed" (231), she is perhaps linked briefly with the drowning Ophelia, whose spreading clothes momentarily support her "mermaid-like" upon the water; like Ophelia, she is engrossed in a fanciful dream-world.[12] "Pensive awhile she dreams awake, and sees, / In fancy, fair St. Agnes in her bed, / But dares not look behind, or all the charm is fled" (232–234). This last line carries a double meaning: in following her ritual, Madeline must look neither "behind, nor sideways" (53); but the real point is that if she did look behind, she would discover Porphyro, and then "the charm" would be "fled" for a more immediate reason.

Asleep in bed, Madeline is said to be "Blissfully haven'd both from joy and pain . . . Blinded alike from sunshine and from rain, / As though a rose should shut, and be a bud again" (240–243). Her dream is "a midnight charm / Impossible to melt as iced stream," "a stedfast spell" (282f., 287). It is while she is in this state of stuporous insensibility—while "still the spell / Unbroken guards her in serene repose," "Still, still she dreams—louder the frost wind blows"—that Porphyro make love to her. On awakening to learn, "No dream, alas! alas! and woe is mine," she calls herself "a deceived thing," echoing Angela's words earlier, "good angels her deceive!" Her condition is pitiful, yet at the same time reprehensible. Her conjuring (perhaps like Merlin's) has backfired upon her, and as hoodwinked dreamer she now gets her reward in coming to face reality a little too late. The rose cannot shut, and be a bud again.

IV

Whether *The Eve of St. Agnes* is a good poem depends in large part on the reader's willingness to find in it a consistency and unity that may not in fact be there.[13] But however it is evaluated, it

---

[12] *Hamlet*, IV. 176–179. This point is made by Stuart M. Sperry, "Madeline and Ophelia," *N&Q*, n. s., IV (1957), 29f.

[13] Keats's conclusion seems a matter for unending debate. The metaphysical critics, remarking that the storm is "an elfin-storm from faery land" and that the lovers "glide, like phantoms" out of the castle, uniformly agree that Madeline and Porphyro transcend mortality, entering an otherworld of eternal felicity, while Angela, the Beadsman, and the warriors remain to die or writhe

stands significantly at the beginning of Keats's single great creative
year, 1819, and it serves to introduce a preoccupation of all the
major poems of this year: that an individual ought not to lose
touch with the realities of this world.

In the poems of 1819, Keats's most explicit, unequivocal statement about the conditions of human life comes in the *Ode on
Melancholy*. Life in the world, we are told in the third stanza, is
an affair in which pleasure and pain are inseparably mixed. Beauty
and the melancholy awareness that beauty must die, joy and the
simultaneous fading of joy, "aching Pleasure" and its instant turn-
ing to poison—all are inextricably bound up in life. There is no
pleasure without pain, and, conversely, if pain is sealed off, so also
is pleasure. One accepts the inseparability of pleasure and pain,
or one rejects life entirely, and suffers a kind of moral and spiritual
emptiness amounting to death. The former is the better alternative:
he lives most fully "whose strenuous tongue / Can burst Joy's grape
against his palate fine."

The first stanza of the ode contains a series of negatives—what
not to do "when the melancholy fit shall fall." Beginning with
forgetfulness, progressing through narcotics to poisons and death,
the images all represent anodynes to escape pain in life. But they

---

benightmared. But the "elfin-storm" is Porphyro's explanation; the narrator
calls it "a tempest fell" of "frost-wind" and "sharp sleet," and other critics (e.g.,
Amy Lowell, *John Keats*, Boston, 1925, II, 175; Herbert G. Wright, "Has Keats's
'Eve of St. Agnes' a Tragic Ending?," *MLR*, XL, 1945, 90–94 [reprinted in this
volume starting on p. oo—ED.] Bernice Slote, *Keats and the Dramatic Principle*,
Lincoln, Neb., 1958, pp. 35f.) have suggested that the lovers face reality, perhaps
even perish, in the storm. Still another view (Wright, p. 92) is that the lovers
face penance in "that second circle of sad hell," the circle of carnal sinners in
the Fifth Canto of the *Inferno*, in which (as Keats described it in his sonnet
"On a Dream") lovers are buffeted about in a storm very much like the one in
"The Eve of St. Agnes." It is possible that Porphyro exists only to the extent
that Madeline is a hoodwinked dreamer, that when she awakens from her dream
the evil represented by him is correspondingly reduced, and a happy human
conclusion is justified. But it seems doubtful, and one may at this point have
to fall back on the remark of the publisher J. A. Hessey, "[Keats] is such a man
of fits and starts he is not much to be depended on" (Edmund Blunden, *Keats's
Publisher*, London, 1936, p. 56), or that of Haydon, "never for two days did he
know his own intentions" (*The Diary of Benjamin Robert Haydon*, ed. Willard
B. Pope, Cambridge, Mass., 1960, II, 317). Whatever the fate of the lovers,
Woodhouse noted that Keats "altered the last 3 lines to leave on the reader a
sense of pettish disgust. . . . He says he likes that the poem should leave off
with this Change of Sentiment" *Letters*, II, 162f).

are rejected, because they shut out pleasure as well as pain, and reduce life to nothing: "For shade to shade will come too drowsily, / And drown the wakeful anguish of the soul." Elsewhere in Keats the anodyne is dreaming, trusting in the visionary imagination, and, to cut short further explanation, the dreamer in the poems of 1819 is always one who would escape pain, but hopes, wrongly, to achieve pleasure. Either he comes to grief through his delusion, or he learns his lesson and wakes up.

Take Madeline as the first instance. In bed, under the delusion that she can achieve bliss in her dream, yet wake up in the virgin morn no weeping Magdalen, she is "Blissfully haven'd both from joy and pain" (240)—for all practical purposes in the narcotic state rejected by the *Ode on Melancholy,* experiencing nothing. Keats reiterates the idea two lines later, "Blinded alike from sunshine and from rain," and the folly of her delusion is represented by the reversal of natural process, "As though a rose should shut, and be a bud again" (242f.). As generally in Keats's poems, dreaming is attended by fairy-tale imagery: under the spell of "faery fancy," Madeline plays the conjuror, and Porphyro is linked in several ways with fairy-lore, witchcraft, and sorcery, as well as pagan sensuality. It is possible that Madeline never completely awakens from her fanciful dream; for she believes Porphyro when he tells her that the storm is "an elfin-storm from faery land" (343), and she imagines "sleeping dragons all around" (353) when they hurry out of the castle.

The heroine of *The Eve of Saint Mark,* written a week or so after the completion of *The Eve of St. Agnes,* in some ways resembles Madeline. Among the "thousand things" perplexing Bertha in the volume she pores over are "stars of Heaven, and angels' wings, / Martyrs in a fiery blaze, / Azure saints in silver rays" (29–32). Enwrapped in the legend of St. Mark, "dazed with saintly imag'ries" (56), she ignores the life in the village around her, and cuts herself off from reality—a "poor cheated soul" (69), "lost in dizzy maze" [14] and mocked by her own shadow.

[14] A variant following line 68 (Garrod, p. 451n.). With Walter E. Houghton's interpretation, "The Meaning of Keats's *Eve of St. Mark,*" *ELH,* XIII (1946), 64–78, I disagree in only one point: that Bertha is a "poor cheated soul" not because she is tied down to the actual, wasting away in oblivion, but because she is cheated by her fancy into denying the actual.

The wretched knight-at-arms in *La Belle Dame sans Merci* is similarly a hoodwinked dreamer. La Belle Dame is "a faery's child"; she sings "A faery's song," speaks "in language strange," and takes him to an "elfin grot." When he awakens from his vision he finds himself "On the cold hill's side." But he is still the dupe of his dream, still hoodwinked, because he continues, in a barren landscape, "Alone and palely loitering," hoping for a second meeting with La Belle Dame. And he denies himself participation in the actual world, which, against his bleak surroundings, is represented as a more fruitful scene, where "The squirrel's granary is full, / And the harvest's done." [15]

In *Lamia*, the hoodwinked dreamer is of course Lycius, who falls in love with the serpent woman Lamia, in whose veins runs "elfin blood," who lingers by the wayside "fairly," with whom he lives in "sweet sin" in a magical palace with a "faery-roof" (I. 147, 200, II. 31, 123). "She seem'd, at once, some penanced lady elf, / Some demon's mistress, or the demon's self" (I. 55f.). What she promises to do for Lycius is what, according to the *Ode on Melancholy*, cannot be done for mortal men: "To unperplex bliss from its neighbour pain; / Define their pettish limits, and estrange / Their points of contact, and swift counterchange." The inseparability of pleasure and pain is for her a "specious chaos"; she will separate them "with sure art" (I. 192–196)—or so the blinded Lycius thinks. But "Spells are but made to break," wrote Keats, in a passage subsequently omitted from the text. "A thrill / Of trumpets" reminds Lycius of the claims of the "noisy world almost forsworn" (II. 27–33), and he holds a wedding feast, at which "cold philosophy," in the form of his old tutor Apollonius, attends to put "all charms" to flight. The "foul dream" Lamia vanishes under the tutor's piercing gaze, and Lycius, too engrossed in his dream to survive, falls dead.

From *Lamia*, we may merely dip into *The Fall of Hyperion* to recall Keats's condemnation of dreamers. They are "vision'ries," "dreamers weak," who seek out wonders, but ignore what is most important, the human face (I. 161–163). "Only the dreamer venoms

---

[15] In my brief treatment of "La Belle Dame" and "Lamia," as in this section of my paper generally, I am indebted to David Perkins's chapters on Keats in *The Quest for Permanence* (Cambridge, Mass., 1959).

all his days" (I. 175), the speaker learns on the steps of Moneta's temple. "The poet and the dreamer are distinct, / Diverse, sheer opposite, antipodes. / The one pours out a balm upon the world, / The other vexes it" (I. 199–202).

Keats's mature view of dreamers illuminates perhaps most importantly the two best odes, on a Grecian Urn and to a Nightingale. In each poem the speaker begins as dreamer, hoodwinked with the idea that he can unperplex bliss from its neighbor pain, that he can find an anodyne to the ills of the flesh by joining the timeless life pictured on an urn, or by fading away into the forest with a bird. In each case the result is an awareness that spells are but made to break: the speaker recognizes the falseness of the dream, the shortcomings of the ideal he has created, and he returns to the mortal world. Life on the urn is at first attractive: unheard melodies are sweeter; the lovers will remain young and fair; the trees will never lose their leaves. Yet it is a static situation, in which life is frozen to a standstill, and there is no fulfillment. Love must be enjoyed, not be stopped forever at a point when enjoyment is just out of reach. The final judgment is that the urn is a "Cold Pastoral," a "friend to man" that, as a work of art, teases him out of thought but offers no possible substitute for life in the actual world.

In the *Ode to a Nightingale,* the speaker would fade away with the bird, and forget "The weariness, the fever, and the fret" of the mortal world, "Where Beauty cannot keep her lustrous eyes, / Or new Love pine at them beyond to-morrow." But when he imaginatively joins the bird in the forest, he immediately longs for the world he has just rejected: "Here there is no light. . . . I cannot see what flowers are at my feet." "In embalmed darkness" he is forced to "guess each sweet" of the transient natural world. As he continues musing, the bird takes on for him the fairy-tale associations that we saw earlier connected with Madeline's dream, La Belle Dame, and Lamia: its immortal voice has charmed "magic casements . . . in faery lands forlorn." The realization that the faery lands are forlorn of human life tolls the dreamer back to his sole self, and he wakes up. The nightingale, symbol of dreams and the visionary imagination, has turned out to be a "deceiving elf." The fancy "cannot cheat so well."

The metaphysical critics are right in asserting Keats's early trust in the imagination. What they sometimes fail to recognize, themselves eager for glimpses of heaven's bourne, and to an extent hoodwinked with their own rather than Keats's metaphysics, is that before Keats wrote more than a handful of poems we would not willingly let die, he in large part changed his mind.[16] Late in January 1818, on sitting down to read *King Lear* once again, he wrote a sonnet bidding goodby to romance: "Let me not wander in a barren dream." A few days later he called it "A terrible division" when the soul is flown upward and the body "earthward press'd. [17] In March he wrote, "It is a flaw / In happiness to see beyond our bourn," and about the same time he recognized that "Four seasons"—not just eternal spring, as the visionary might conjure up—"Four seasons fill the measure of the year." Similarly "There are four seasons in the mind of man," who "has his Winter too of pale misfeature, / Or else he would forego his mortal nature." [18] In July, on his walking trip to Scotland, he wrote:

> Scanty the hour and few the steps beyond the bourn of care,
> Beyond the sweet and bitter,—beyond the bourn of care,
> Scanty the hour and few the steps, because a longer stay
> Would bar return, and make a man forget his mortal way:
> O horrible! to lose the sight of well remember'd face. . . .
> No, no, that horror cannot be, for at the cable's length
> Man feels the gentle anchor pull and gladdens in its strength.[19]

It is the gentle anchor of mortality that ties us to the world; man gladdens in its strength. "Fancy," said Keats to Reynolds, "is indeed less than a present palpable reality." It would be a distortion of fact to maintain that he always held this later view, but it is

[16] Glen O. Allen, "The Fall of Endymion: A Study in Keats's Intellectual Growth," *K-SJ*, VI (1957), 37–57, argues authoritatively that the change occurred during the winter of 1817–18, while Keats was completing and revising *Endymion*. Ford, p. 141, acknowledges the change, but connects it with *La Belle Dame*, and thereafter discusses among important poems only *Lamia*. Perkins, p. 220, feels that "the over-all course of . . . [Keats's] development might be partly described as a periodic, though gradually cumulative, loss of confidence in the merely visionary imagination."

[17] "God of the Meridian."

[18] "To J. H. Reynolds, Esq.," ll. 82f.; "Four Seasons."

[19] "Lines Written in the Highlands after a Visit to Burns's Country," ll. 29–33, 39f.

worth noting that even when he and his fancy could not agree, he declared himself "more at home amongst Men and women," happier reading Chaucer than Ariosto.[20]

The dreamer in Keats is ultimately one who turns his back, not merely on the pains of life, but on life altogether; and in the poems of 1819, beginning with *The Eve of St. Agnes,* his dreaming is condemned. If the major concern in these poems is the conflict between actuality and the ideal, the result is not a rejection of the actual, but rather a facing-up to it that amounts, in the total view, to affirmation. It is a notable part of Keats's wisdom that he never lost touch with reality, that he condemned his hoodwinked dreamers who would shut out the world, that he recognized life as a complexity of pleasure and pain, and laid down a rule for action: achievement of the ripest, fullest experience that one is capable of. These qualities make him a saner if in some ways less romantic poet than his contemporaries, and they should qualify him as the Romantic poet most likely to survive in the modern world.

[20] *Letters,* I, 325, II, 234.

The Winter of 1818–19

by Walter Jackson Bate

It was early January now. *Hyperion* still was not going ahead.
The two "rondeaus" had not seemed to help. What writing he has
done over the past few weeks, as he tells Haydon (January 10), is
"nothing to speak of." He feels as though he were "moulting,"
and is chronically discontented with himself in the process. Meanwhile Haydon is prepared for Keats's loan—"I now frankly tell
you," Haydon has just written, "I will accept your friendly offer."
Haydon's only hopes of surmounting "the concluding difficulties
of my Picture lie in *you*." Keats, in reply, declares that he will
do what he can, and "do not let there be any mention of interest."

On January 18 or 19 he went to Chichester, joining Brown at
the home of Dilke's parents. These gentle, elderly people knew all
about Tom's lingering illness and death and about George's de-
parture, and were prepared to exert themselves to make the time
as pleasant as possible. Brown, who liked elderly people when
they were themselves kindly, had already brought gusto and what
he considered to be humor into the household. Hoping to distract
Keats, he tried even harder after his friend's arrival. He was constantly clowning. Miss Sarah Mullins—a pleasant woman in her
seventies with whom Brown pretended to be flirting—had persuaded him to shave off his whiskers. They all laughed at the
change, and told Brown that he looked like a woman. Eager to
oblige, the burly Brown appeared at breakfast wearing old Mrs.

"*The Winter of 1818–19*" by Walter Jackson Bate. *From* John Keats (*Cambridge: Harvard University Press, 1963), pp. 436–51. Reprinted by permission
of The Belknap Press of Harvard University Press. Copyright © 1963 by the
President and Fellows of Harvard College. Abridged by permission of the publisher.*

Dilke's hood and talking in a high feminine voice. Thus these four or five days passed, and on two evenings they all went out together, said Keats, "to old Dowager card parties," which would last until ten o'clock.

But throughout the visit he was brooding on the need to start writing something, and, as if in a gesture of determination, had brought with him the paper (several thin sheets that William Saslam had given him) on which he had been jotting down his long letter to George and Georgiana. Within a day or so he began to think more seriously of the suggestion of Isabella Jones that he write on the legend of St. Agnes' Eve (the Eve itself was January 20); and he may even have made a start on the poem. He and Brown then walked the thirteen miles to Bedhampton (January 23) in order to stay with John Snook and his wife, Dilke's brother-in-law and sister, at their house, which still stands (the Old Mill House).[1] Here, during the next nine or ten days, Keats wrote the *Eve of St. Agnes,* averaging about thirty-five to forty lines a day. He scarcely left the house except when they all went (January 25) to see the dedication of a chapel built by Lewis Way, a wealthy man who had just bought Stansted Park (a huge estate of 5,500 acres near Bedhampton) and had decided to turn it into a sort of college for the conversion of the Jews to Christianity.[2] The day afterwards, Brown returned to Hampstead. Keats stayed

[1] For discussion, see Guy Murchie, *The Spirit of Place in Keats* (1955), pp. 141–151.

[2] A full account of Way and of the dedication of the chapel is given by Robert Gittings, *John Keats: The Living Year* (Barnes & Noble, 1968), pp. 75–82, who persuasively points out (pp. 87–89) the connection of images in lines 30–38 of the *Eve of St. Mark* with the Stansted Chapel. An interesting possibility is a connection between some of the detail in the windows and that in the casement stanza of the *Eve of St. Agnes* (pp. 79–81). But here the shapes and colors, however sumptuously Keats describes them, are conventional. If we stress particular sources, an equally good possibility would be the parish church at Enfield which Keats had seen so frequently at an impressionable age. Not only the large central window over the altar (a source of some local pride at the time) but the ten large side windows were "triple-arched." At that time, beneath the central rose window, were also two large diamond-shaped windows, each of them subdivided into four smaller diamonds. Knights were shown on one side and "ladies praying" on another; "shielded scutcheons" and "heraldries" were in all of the windows. For an engraving and descriptions, see William Robinson, *History and Antiquities of Enfield* (1823), II.5, 25–30. For various figures on tombs, some now removed, cf. II.32, 41–56.

on for another five days (until February 1 or 2), having caught
another sore throat in the meantime. Probably by the time he returned, the *Eve of St. Agnes* was finished. . . .

The poem takes the special (but still relatively simple) form
that it does partly because of the ways in which Keats's growing un-
easiness with the romance as a genre and his intention of writing
something different from the "mawkish" *Isabella* continue to op-
erate against—and yet are constantly being modified by—the descriptive and musical richness of setting. And in speaking of the
setting (so frankly—and so successfully—important an element
in the poem), the peculiar opportunities and limitations of the
Spenserian stanza itself should be kept in mind. "Mrs. Tighe and
Beattie," he wrote George shortly before he began the poem, "once
delighted me—now I see through them and can find nothing in
them—or weakness." And, as if in a spirit of open challenge, he
selected the same verse form they themselves had used, the Spenserian stanza, though he was altogether unpracticed in it and in
fact had hardly used it except in his first poem (the four-stanza
"Imitation of Spenser"), written back in the Edmonton surgery.
But of course there were also good formal arguments for using
the stanza; and the mere fact that it was chosen, and that he began
to exploit its opportunities so quickly, contributes in turn to the
character of the poem. To begin with, the stanza is capacious
enough not to pinch the writer into the affectations of compression
that *ottava rima* so frequently does, as Keats himself had found
in *Isabella*. Yet at the same time it is very much of a unit. The result is that it tempts poetic narrative toward tableau, ample and
yet self-contained. The musical potentiality of the stanza's structure is analogous in its effect, permitting massiveness while it also
compels unity (unity, that is, within each individual stanza). For
the central recurring rhyme (the *b*-rhyme of *a b a b b c b c c*) can
sustain as well as interlock, continuing to act as a kind of sounding
board until the reverberation is lost in the long wave of the concluding six-foot line. There were opportunities, then—however
specialized because of the nature of the verse form—for the co-
alescence of economy and richness that distinguishes his style generally from *Hyperion* through the odes. And this characteristic,
from the first stanza, further helps to set the *Eve of St. Agnes*

(whatever it lacks otherwise) apart from every other romance in English.

Within this context of musical and pictorial setting appear characters by no means idealized (at least one of the two principal ones being somewhat deluded about his own motives). But they— like the seduction itself—are either elevated or else protectively muffled as one haunting stanza majestically concludes and makes way for another. The situation was in every way fertile for what, if he had not thought of it very explicitly before he started, quickly became a distingushing quality once the poem began, that is, the ebb and flow of emerging contrasts and partial resolutions, such as the advanced age and frailty of the two minor characters and the youth of the lovers; the temporary inner warmth and the all-enveloping cold; music and silence; the interplay of the religious and the erotic, which Keats caught from *Romeo and Juliet;* and even the divided reactions within the characters themselves (notably Porphyro, who is touched to tears at the thought of Madeline's innocent trust in the legend of St. Agnes' Eve and yet at the same time evolves his ruse to take advantage of it). The apex is reached when the central episode builds on Keats's familiar theme of dreaming and waking.

The aged Beadsman is the first—and he returns to be the last— of the characters that move both with and against the "coloring" and "drapery" that Keats felt to be the principal merit of the poem if it had any:

> St. Agnes' Eve—Ah, bitter chill it was!
> The owl, for all his feathers, was a-cold;
> The hare limp'd trembling through the frozen grass,
> And silent was the flock in woolly fold:
> Numb were the Beadsman's fingers, while he told
> His rosary, and while his frosted breath,
> Like pious incense from a censer old,
> Seem'd taking flight for heaven, without a death,
> Past the sweet Virgin's picture, while his prayer he saith.

"Meagre, barefoot, wan," he rises from his knees and walks down the freezing chapel aisle past the "sculptur'd dead." One thinks of the phrase Keats so liked in Shakespeare's sonnets: "death's eternal cold." As the Beadsman passes those long-dead knights and ladies forever "Emprison'd in black, purgatorial rails," the "weak spirit" of this frail man is touched with sharp sympathy "To think how they may ache in icy hoods and mails." The poignance is put briefly as the soft prelude of the music comes to him from the hall:

> Northward he turneth through a little door,
> And scarce three steps, ere Music's golden tongue
> Flatter'd to tears this aged man and poor.

But with the habits of a lifetime he turns from the music:

> His was harsh penance on St. Agnes' Eve:
> Another way he went, and soon among
> Rough ashes sat he for his soul's reprieve,
> And all night kept awake, for sinners' sake to grieve.

Like his counterpart, the aged nurse Angela, he will shortly die; and the implication at the end of the poem—gentle, not labored— is that his death is nothing to be admired but only the inevitable falling of a leaf before the winter of fact.[3] Meanwhile, in the hall, the soft prelude fades, and the "silver, snarling trumpets" begin to "chide" as if in response to the throng of guests who now burst in, their brains "stuff'd" with expectations of romance. Above the chiding trumpets and fluctuating life,

> The carvéd angels, ever eager-ey'd
> Star'd, where upon their heads the cornice rests,
> With hair blown back, and wings put cross-wise on
> their breasts.

Another contrast begins to emerge. The innocent Madeline, her own brain "stuff'd" with the legends she has "heard old dames"

---

[3] Nothing shows more graphically Keats's later reaction to the poem (September) than his impetuously harsh and flippant revision of the last three lines of the poem:

> Angela went off
> Twitch'd by the palsy—and with face deform
> The Beadsman stiffen'd—twixt a sigh and laugh
> Ta'en sudden from his beads by one weak little cough.

Woodhouse said that he wanted the poem to "leave off with this Change of Sentiment—it was what he aimed at, & was glad to find from by objections to it that he had succeeded" (II.163).

tell her about St. Agnes's Eve, is preparing to keep it with literal
fidelity: by following certain rituals and going supperless to bed,
she will see in dream her future husband. "Full of this whim," she
fails to notice the suitors who approach; "The music, yearning like
a God in pain, / She scarcely heard." She is "Hoodwink'd with
faery fancy; all amort, / Save to St. Agnes and her lambs unshorn."
But an atmosphere of hatred permeates the castle and threatens
this stir of love. Like Juliet or Isabella, she is surrounded by a
family at mortal feud with that of the man she hopes to wed.

Meanwhile, eager to catch some glimpse of Madeline, the young
Porphyro has ridden across the wintry moors, and, like Romeo,
enters a festive hall fraught with danger. His only possible help is
Angela, Madeline's aged nurse—considerably less staunch than
Juliet's nurse. Her palsied frailty is made almost ludicrous: she has
not only a "dizzy head" but "agues in her brain" (at the close of
the poem she dies "palsy-twitch'd"). But, like the Beadsman, she
is always being assimilated by the atmosphere against which she
begins to move in contrast. The potentially grotesque gestures are
softened, as when she cackles at Madeline's gullible trust in the
dream to come ("Feebly she laugheth in the languid moon") or
falls into senile mutter as she leads Porphyro to a place where his
enemies will not find him:

> He follow'd through a lowly archèd way,
> Brushing the cobwebs with his lofty plume,
> And as she mutter'd "Well-a-well-a-day!"
> He found him in a little moonlight room,
> Pale, lattic'd, chill, and silent as a tomb.

As Angela tells him of Madeline's hope for a vision, Porphyro is
both touched and also inspired with a plan: Angela is to take him
secretly to Madeline's chamber, hide him in a closet from which he
can look out, and bring fruits for a feast he will spread. He will
then sing and awaken Madeline, and she will see the future husband of whom she has been dreaming. Angela is understandably
shocked at the proposal (he is "wicked" and "impious," not at all
the same person that he had seemed). But Porphyro swears his
intentions are good, and is indeed himself convinced that they are
("Good Angela, believe me by these tears"); and he then impul-

sively threatens that he otherwise will shout until his enemies in
the castle discover him. The threat further unnerves the palsied
Angela. The mercurial Porphyro seems a little ashamed; and he
begins to speak with "such deep sorrowing" that Angela agrees and
leads him to Madeline's chamber.

His spirits again raised, the ardent lover takes "covert" before
Madeline (a "ring-dove") enters:

> Now prepare,
> Young Porphyro, for gazing on that bed.

Keats is recalling the famous scene in *Cymbeline* where the evil
Iachimo conceals himself in order to look on Imogen while she
sleeps; even some of the phrasing is echoed. Keats's young impul-
sive lover is by no means a Iachimo. But his actions are far from
those of the heroes in the romances Keats and Felton Mathew
("the valiant Eric") had once read, and far from what we should
have expected from the decorous Lorenzo in *Isabella*.[4] In any case
the atmosphere once again pervades and modifies; and at this cru-
cial moment it does so dramatically—through the effect, that is,
on Porphyro himself. For immediately after Madeline enters the
room, the magnificent stanza (xxiv) on the triple-arched casement
follows. The rich interplay of color into which the protecting
casement turns the cold moonlight not only shelters the undressing
of Madeline but, as she kneels to pray, also serves to shake once
again Porphyro's single-mindedness:

> Rose-bloom fell on her hands, together prest,
> And on her silver cross soft amethyst,
> And on her hair a glory . . .
> . . . Porphyro grew faint:
> She knelt, so pure a thing, so free from mortal taint.

Now and in the next few stanzas Porphyro is feeling that he is
in something very like a "paradise." But the word has been over-
stressed in discussions of the poem. For the quasi-religious imagery
that follows the casement stanza significantly subsides, and, with
one minor exception, is confined throughout the remaining 150

---

[4] For a perceptive discussion of Porphyro's character, and indeed the entire
poem, see J. C. Stillinger, *Studies in Philology*, LVIII (1961), 533–555 [reprinted
in this volume starting on p. 49—ED.].

lines of the poem to only two remarks by Porphyro himself (one of which, that he is a "famish'd pilgrim,—saved by miracle," by no means describes honestly to Madeline the calculated "stratagem" by which he has arrived). We go too far, in other words, when we equate the religious and the erotic in this poem. A remark that Keats wrote in his copy of the *Anatomy of Melancholy* is relevant: "nothing disgraces me in my own eyes so much as being one of a race of eyes nose and mouth beings" who "have always mingled goatish winnyish lustful love with the abstract adoration of the deity." The "paradise," in other words, is altogether subjective, within Porphyro himself. Nor is it a paradise to him solely because the erotic is frankly reinforcing itself—as any passion tends to do— by incorporating other feelings. Rather he has been genuinely struck by a diversity of impressions, all of them strong (and they also include fear and guilt: he has "stol'n" here; he "creeps" from the closet). This very diversity of impression, in effect, numbs him. In a specialized way, and applied to a particular character, we have an anticipation of the "numbness" (the "being too happy") that later provides a beginning to the "Ode to a Nightingale": the "yearning" or "aching" that fills the mind comes not in the satis- faction of a single emotion ("Where's the cheek that doth not fade, / Too much gaz'd at?" he had written in the lines on "Fancy") but in the active interplay of diverse feelings still in the process of working toward resolution and "winning near the goal." Creeping from the closet and dreading discovery, Porphyro, "half-anguish'd," lays the table for a feast, and then beseeches Madeline to awake, "Or I shall drowse beside thee, so my soul doth ache." But in his faintness he is really only "whispering." His arm goes about her; she does not awaken. Finally he pulls himself away, takes his lute, and sings the ballad "La belle dame sans mercy" close to her ear. Her eyes open.

But Madeline's partial awakening from the dream is far from reassuring. In this almost deliberate variation of Adam's dream ("he awoke and found it truth"), she finds the sight of Porphyro a "painful change": the dream has proved to be more attractive than the reality. These are "sad eyes" that now look at her, while those in her vision had been "spiritual and clear." The figure next to her is, in comparison, "pallid, chill": where are those "looks immortal"? The play of dream and reality is thus built into the plot. But we strain at the poem when we assume that, because of Keats's more serious use of it elsewhere, it carries an equally heavy symbolic weight at all times. It is natural for a writer to be attracted to similar situations, and especially to have recourse to them when the action is slight, when the poem is written swiftly, and when his attention (as is very much the case in this poem) is particularly concentrated on idiom and versification. But the context at least allows us to note one relatively simple but recurring thought of Keats which is to become more prominent in the poetry of 1819: a dream—like innocence—cannot be lived in the world without being violated; and yet, whatever is lost, actual happiness is impossible without an awakening from dream to reality. At all events, the dream again completely absorbs the half-asleep Madeline. The first version—and also the one finally printed—then moves with quick delicacy. "Beyond a mortal man impassion'd far," the lover rises from his knees:

> Into her dream he melted, as the rose
> Blendeth its odour with the violet,—
> Solution sweet.[5]

But the finality of what has happened is plain. "St. Agnes' moon hath set," and the storm outside immediately rises. Completely awakening, Madeline realizes her situation. ("No dream, alas!"; she is "a deceivèd thing"; a "traitor" has brought Porphyro here; what if he now forsakes her?) Protesting the integrity of his love, assuring her that they will wed, he instinctively capitalizes on her desire for the continuation of the magic of St. Agnes' Eve and on his own half-conviction that he has been "sav'd by miracle": this

[5] It is here that Keats made the revision to which Woodhouse especially objected, adding that, if in the previous version "there was an opening for doubt what took place, it was [Keats's own] fault for not writing clearly." Woodhouse told Taylor that "This alteration is of about 3 stanzas." The surviving copy involves only part of two stanzas. The close of stanza xxxv (where Madeline says simply "Oh leave me not in this eternal woe, / For if thou diest, my Love, I know not where to go") was temporarily changed to "See while she speaks his arms encroaching slow / Have zon'd her, heart to heart—loud, loud the dark winds blow." Then stanza xxxvi (which in the published version was printed as above) emphasizes more specifically that Madeline is asleep, describes her dream as "wild," omits the saccharine phrase "solution sweet," and stresses the sudden rise of the storm. . . .

rising storm outside, he says, is elf-inspired for their escape; ("an elfin-storm from faery land / Of haggard seeming, but a boon indeed"). And the poem ends with no warm, confident response from Madeline. "She hurried at his words, beset with fears." The apprehensive lovers "glide, like phantoms, into the wide hall," through the castle, quietly slipping the bolts, one by one. Nor is there any assurance that they survived:

> And they are gone: ay, ages long ago
> These lovers fled away into the storm.

That night the Baron and his warrior guests were plagued with troubled dreams; Angela died; and

> The Beadsman, after thousand aves told,
> For aye unsought for slept among his ashes cold.

* * *

The result is a poem begun with mixed and even negative feelings (including fatigue and grief, the need to keep his mind occupied in this trying time, thoughts of Fanny Brawne, acute anxiety about his inability to continue *Hyperion,* and the determination not to revert to another *Isabella*), and yet a poem that at the same time turns into a feat of craftsmanship—a triumph of idiom and versification over the limitations of the subject—because the new artistry he had gained through *Hyperion* was freshly and yet very simply challenged. It is no accident that the most complete worksheet we have of any of Keats's poems is the first draft of the *Eve of St. Agnes.* Because he was working rapidly, he used the same copy instead of making successive drafts; and he made his changes line by line as he was writing his first draft, sometimes fumbling and sometimes leaping toward more effective expression. Rarely in any poem after *Endymion* has he ever written a phrase that can be compared in flatness and banality to those that frequently begin a stanza, a line, or a sentence, as he writes the *Eve of St. Agnes.* The poem as such is by no means absorbing him. Yet immediately, as soon as the phrase is jotted down, his judgment is piqued, and he alters and then, with quick exasperation, alters again.[6] Some are

[6] A full discussion of the manuscript revisions is given in M. R. Ridley, *Keats' Craftsmanship* (1933), pp. 112–190. I merely summarize a few examples from Mr. Ridley's detailed and perceptive analysis.

amusing. At least one is also a little poignant. "Have you some
warm furs?" he had asked George and Georgiana in December.
And the following year, when he becomes so ill, the constant chilli-
ness turns into an obsession: in letter after letter he tells both his
sister and Fanny Brawne: "Be very careful to wear warm clothing
in a thaw"; "Be very careful of open doors and windows and going
without your duffle grey"; "Remember to be very careful of your
cloathing." Now, as Porphyro rouses Madeline at the close of the
poem to prepare to flee into the storm ("the morning is at hand, /
The bloated wassailers will never heed, / Let us away . . ."),
Keats finds himself, at first, impulsively writing "Put on warm
cloathing sweet, and fearless be." The most involved of all his
struggles, and one accompanied by abysmal plunges, is with the
stanza on Madeline's preparation for bed (xxvi). The near-comedy
of the struggle and Keats's growing exasperation can be followed
only when the writing of the whole of the stanza is followed step
by step in Mr. Ridley's account.[7] From it we may select just a few
moments. In the final version, the stanza begins:

> Anon his heart revives: her vespers done,
> Of all its wreathèd pearls her hair she frees;
> Unclasps her warmèd jewels one by one;
> Loosens her fragrant boddice; by degrees
> Her rich attire creeps rustling to her knees.

But Keats, when he first started it, got himself into various trou-
bles, one of which is an unwanted intrusion of abrupt motion—
Madeline virtually pulls her headdress from her hair:

> But soon his heart revives—her prayers said
> She [lays aside her veil]   pearled
>   Stript her hair of all it ∧ wreathed [pearl]
> Unclasps her bosom jewels

He is far from satisfied as he writes this, and least of all with the
line he next jots down in trying to get a rhyme for "said": "And
twists it in one knot upon her head." Beginning all over, and
gradually improving those lines, he enters the next part of the
stanza with uncertainty, "Loosens her boddice from her . . . ,"

[7] Pp. 153–156.

crosses it out, and goes through the following changes, "Loosens her Boddice lace string," "Loosens her Boddice and her bosom bare," and (something hard to explain except that he is probably rather flurried with exasperation) "Loosens her bursting boddice." Clearing this up, he goes on and pictures her "Half hidden like a Syren of the Sea." Recalling that the association with "sirens" has an unpleasant side, he finally replaces it with:

> by degrees
> Her rich attire creeps rustling to her knees:
> Half-hidden like a mermaid in sea-weed.

To follow out an entire stanza briefly, we can take that on the casement (xxiv). Keats begins, "A casement ach'd" (as usual, when writing rapidly, he is forgetting his *r*'s), crosses out "a[r]ch'd," and elaborates:

> A Casement ⟨ach'd⟩ tripple arch'd and diamonded
> With many coloured glass fronted the Moon
> In midst ⟨of which⟩ wereof a shilded scutcheon shed
> High blushing gules, upon

The light is to fall on Madeline. But in the previous stanza she has only just entered the door, full of excitement. Needing first to have things calmed and stationed a bit, he crosses out "upon," and writes:

> a shilded scutcheon shed
> High blushing gules: she kneeled saintly down
> And inly prayed for grace and heavenly boon;
> The blood red gules fell on her silver cross
> And her white hands devout.

The last half line is especially bald; and, while hesitating generally about the whole stanza, he crosses out "her," altering the phrase to "And whitest hands devout."

Here, hastily put together, is some raw material. And Keats, as Mr. Ridley says, "takes it all to pieces," and "begins to put the fragments together in a different design," postponing Madeline until later and focusing more on the casement itself. He crosses out all that he has written and starts afresh (forgetting his *r*'s again in "triple"), inserts "There was" at the beginning, and goes on:

> There was a Casement tipple archd and high
> All garlanded with carven imageries
> Of fruits & trailing flowers and sunny corn.

But the third line lacks rhyme. He crosses out "trailing," and makes the line read "Of fruits & flowers and sunny corn ears parch'd" (the final two words are far from satisfactory; but the problem of rhyme is on his mind for the moment; and he is thinking of changing the first line to end "high and triple-arch'd"). Then suddenly, after this tinkering, he feels that a breakthrough is coming. He again crosses out everything he has done, and writes so rapidly that his word "garlanded" is momentarily lost in this garden of flowers and fruits, and he puts down "gardneded":

> A Casement high and tripple archd there was
> All gardneded with carven imageries
> Of fruits and flowers and bunches of knot grass;
> And diamonded with panes of quaint device
> Innumerable of stains and splendid dies
> As is the wing of evening tiger moths;
> And in the midst 'mong ⟨man⟩ thousand heraldries
> And dim twilight

Separating "dim" and "twilight" he ends the stanza:

> And twilight saints and nim emblazonings
> A shielded scutcheon blushd with Blood of Queens and Kings.

To get a rhyme for "Kings" and "emblazonings" he must now change the final word in the line "As is the wing of evening tiger moths." He writes above it, "As is the tiger moths rich," crosses out "rich" and writes "deep damasked wings," hesitates about "damasked," and writes "sunset" above it ("deep sunset wings"), and so leaves it, though returning in the final version to "As are the tiger-moth's deep-damask'd wings":

> A casement high and triple-arch'd there was,
> All garlanded with craven imag'ries
> Of fruits, and flowers, and bunches of knot-grass,
> And diamonded with panes of quaint device,
> Innumerable of stains and splendid dyes,
> As are the tiger-moth's deep-damask'd wings;

And in the midst, 'mong thousand heraldries,
And twilight saints, and dim emblazonings,
A shielded scutcheon blush'd with blood of queens and kings.

To sum up, nothing else that he wrote shows so much the un-
leashed freedom with which the technique of composition can
itself become a dominant emotion. Keats was enough of a disciple
of Hazlitt not to take seriously any thought that concern with technique alone can lift the artist above apprentice writing. (Was
Titian, said Hazlitt, "when he painted a landscape, . . . pluming
himself on being thought the finest colourist in the world, or making himself so by looking at nature"?) In fact one rarely creates
or discovers technique—a means to an end—except by trying to
do something besides employ technique for its own sake. But
larger challenges were not what Keats required at the moment. Because of the daily distress of nursing Tom, he had hurried himself
prematurely into beginning *Hyperion*. Yet much that he had
learned through *Hyperion* remained, as it were, in suspension—
all the readier for use because the original hope was frustrated, at
least for the time being. He later spoke slightingly of the "colouring" and "drapery" of the *Eve of St. Agnes*. Of course he would
have ideally preferred "a Poem in which Character and Sentiment
would be the figures to such drapery." But in this altogether necessary respite, everything worked temporarily toward "drapery" or
tapestry, including the mere existence of a new ability in weaving
it and a welcome brief freedom from such subjects he felt to be substantial and demanding.

Rich Antiquity

by Robert Gittings

Bertha was a Maiden fair,
Dwelling in the old Minster square:
From her fireside she could see
Sidelong its rich antiquity.
    —The Eve of St. Mark

A week or ten days before his long-deferred visit to Chichester, Keats had told Haydon, "I have been writing a little now and then lately; but nothing to speak of—being discontented and as it were moulting—." He was in a state of dissatisfaction with his poetry, though it did not provoke the violent reaction of his apprentice days when such a state made him think of suicide. Keats had learnt since then that such moods were often the prelude to a step forward. It is a measure of the distance he had travelled in the few years since he began poetry that he now made a joke of suicide. "Yet I do not think," he added to Haydon, "I shall ever come to the rope or the Pistol." He had learnt to make a medicine of his moods of depression. "I see by little and little more of what is to be done, and how it is to be done, should I ever be able to do it," and half-humourously he added, "On my Soul there should be some reward for that continual 'agonie ennuiyeuse.'" Going through his box of books had reminded him of his early reading and his own early writing. The poets who had influenced him then, like Beattie and Tighe, now seemed nothing as he reread them; he himself, he felt, had progressed, but there was still so much to be done. It was a

"Rich Antiquity" by Robert Gittings. From John Keats *(Boston: Little, Brown and Company; London: Heineman Educational Books, Ltd., 1968), pp. 275–85. Reprinted by permission of Little, Brown and Company and Heinemann Educational Books Ltd. Copyright © 1968 by Robert Gittings.*

fruitful mood for a new leap forward in poetry, but so far he had been able to do nothing but tinker. He seems to have tried some revisions on *Hyperion*, but with Keats it was always difficult to re-start a poem that had gone cold on him. In his present mood he needed a new shift of view to release the smothered poetic energy within him.

Keats was always affected by a change of scene. While writing the first book of *Endymion*, he had been oppressed by the isolation of the Isle of Wight, disturbed by the bleak landscape at Margate, and had dashed to Canterbury to strike inspiration out of its as-sociation with *The Canterbury Tales*. He deliberately exploited places for poetry—"to look into some beautiful Scenery—for poeti-cal purposes"—and his epic mountain tour had been undertaken for the purposes of writing an epic. Neither Brown's gossip nor Dilke's letters, however, could have told him how exactly Chichester and what he found there would strike the note he was now un-consciously seeking. The very approach, as the coach bumpily de-scended the long chalk trackway from the South Downs, carried him into warmer more welcoming climate than the bare cragginess he had sought in Scotland and imported into the primeval background of the Titans. This coastal plain, where corn ripens earlier than anywhere else in England, creates an instant atmosphere of well-being. The city itself had risen from Civil War and siege, which had left it still in an almost ruinous state only a hundred years be-fore, to an urbane prosperity. This was reflected in the warm red-brick Georgian houses, "new-built," as their deeds described them, by the merchants who derived their fat profits from the Govern-ment bounty on the export of corn. From upper windows or bel-vederes, the owners could see their grain-ships moving on the long haul out of the creeks of Chichester Harbour as if they sailed along the flat fertile land. Elderly people who had profited in the locality retired here, in solid comfort. Keats's hosts were such a couple in just such a house. Charles Wentworth Dilke senior, during his career in the Navy Office, had dealt with merchants and corn-factors of the coastal plain between Chichester and Portsmouth. One of these, John Snook of Portsea, acquired a mill at Bedhamp-ton. Business naturally led to personal association, for Dilke's daughter Laetitia had married Snook's son, John the second, who had just taken over the mill on his father's death. The elder Dilke had by now himself retired, and for the last five years he and his wife had lived among the older society of Chichester, in a house looking out over the orchards that still came up to the city walls. It was to these two households, the elderly Civil Servant and his wife and the miller, a stout figure out of Chaucer, that Keats was bidden. To someone who had been completely on his own, fending for himself in the presence of death and continual doubts, this was a warm refuge of relief.

When he got off the coach in the middle of the city, met by the ebullient Brown with a torrent of provincial gossip, Keats instantly came upon a new sight that seemed like an answer to his poetic mood. All his reading in the past few weeks had thrown him back into the romantic and Gothic, to the medieval rather than the classic, to Chatterton and Spenser rather than to Milton and Wordsworth. As he walked through the streets with Brown back to their hosts, the Cathedral sprang straight from the streets above them, on the citizens' doorsteps, its separate bell-tower with the circling jackdaws actually fronting the road itself. Unlike Canterbury, it was almost all as it had been in the early middle ages, a building of one character hardly altered in 600 years, except that clear glass showed where the Roundheads had smashed the coloured diamonding with their pikes. For one in a romantic and Gothic mood, here was a setting come to life; and as Keats was drawn by Brown into the elderly card-playing circle of their hosts, "old Dowager card parties" as he wrote to George, he found that these ancient ladies lived among even more ancient and medieval prospects, rooms dating from the middle ages with winding stone stairs and pointed windows, cellars with broad Norman supporting pillars. The Georgian facade, in houses in the midst of the city, often concealed a far older period of history.

So, as Keats sat and played cards with old Mrs. Lacy and old Miss Mullins,[1] while Brown, who had a way with elderly ladies, fluttered and teased their hostesses, the beginnings of the medieval setting of the new poem took shape. Yet this scene, though immediate and actual, and reproduced in early stanzas of *The Eve of St.*

[1] *Letters*, II, 34; *John Keats: The Living Year*, 69–72.

Agnes with their broad hall-pillars, lowly arched ways, and little moonlight room, was only an incidental spark to set light to the piled-up material within him. So too, for all the help that she undoubtedly intended to him, was Isabella Jones's suggestion that he should write, this St. Agnes Eve, a poem on the theme of the legend. Keats's mind was already prepared to go far beyond and behind the simple superstition

> how, upon St. Agnes' Eve,
> Young virgins might have visions of delight,
> And soft adorings from their loves receive
> Upon the honey'd middle of the night.

A much more tangible love-story was working below the surface of his mind. It was brought to light by Isabella—perhaps even by his own situation with her—and by the rich and evocative medieval ambiance which now surrounded him. Keats made the central part of his poem differ from the folk-lore tale. It was not a vision his heroine received, but the physical presence of her love, who had found his way into her room to see her sleeping. Either by design or by a lucky accident, he had been reading a small volume of tales in French, which all had the common property of a young man introduced, by varying means, into a beautiful young woman's rooms, a love-affair and an elopement. It seems probable that this was the volume on which he had hoped to base the prose story, never written, which he had promised to send George. The book consisted of three romances collected and written by M. de Tressan and published in Paris just over thiry years earlier, the ninth volume of the *Bibliothèque Universelle des Dames: Romans.* These romances were entitled *Flores et Blanche-Fleur, Cléomades et Claremonde,* and *Pierre de Provence et La Belle Maguelone.* Plot, setting and descriptive detail from all three combine to make them the undoubted source for the dramatic plan of Keats's poem.[2]

Although the first story of the group, in Boccaccio's Italian version and under the more familiar title of *Il Filocolo,* has been conjectured to have prompted Keats, it was a combination of all three stories, and especially the last-named on which he drew. Pierre and

---

[2] I am indebted for this suggestion to Dr. J. H. Walter, who has very generously placed his unpublished notes at my disposal.

Maguelone become, as even their names might suggest, Keats's
Porphyro and Madeline. Many small details in the story are the
same, or similar. The setting is a palace or castle where festivities
are taking place, with a small chapel adjoining; an old nurse helps
the lovers to meet after satisfying herself on the hero's intentions;
there is a reference to "un chanson de son pays"—that is, the hero's
country of Provence—echoed by Keats's Porphyro when

> He play'd an ancient ditty, long since mute,
> In Provence call'd, "La belle dame sans mercy:"

and finally when the lovers elope there is a storm, which, in the
French romance, delays their story's happy ending by separating
them. Other elements which Keats used as stage-properties come
from the other two stories in the same little volume. The hero in
the first story finds entry through a basket of fruits and flowers, in
the second he wanders through a feast, both of which may have
helped Keats to introduce the entirely new incident of a luxurious
feast into the original legend of St. Agnes Eve. Similarly the immediate elopement, long-delayed in *Pierre et Maguelone,* is a part
of the companion-piece of *Cléomades et Claremonde,* as is the
sprawling figure of the Porter, which Keats transmuted into an un-
forgettable accompaniment to the escape of the lovers:

> They glide, like phantoms, into the wide hall;
> Like phantoms, to the iron porch, they glide;
> Where lay the Porter, in uneasy sprawl,
> With a huge empty flagon by his side:

These stories too, with their Mediterranean settings, which include adventures among the Moors of North Africa, foreshadow
much of Keats's imagery in the poem, which contains a counterpoint throughout of Christian and pagan, such as his description of
the sleeping Madeline

> Clasp'd like a missal where swart Paynims pray;

and the oriental luxuries of the feast Porphyro brings her.

Yet however much these romances may have settled Keats in
the plot-form of his own love-story, the poetic texture of the poem
is far too thickly woven to depend on any one literary source. More

than perhaps in any other single poem, Keats brings to the actual working-out of the verse in *The Eve of St. Agnes* the fruits of an intense, though short lifetime of reading; he is his own poetic Porphyro, gathering together the most diversely-varied contributions to the feast, from Coleridge's *Christabel* to the romances of Mrs. Ann Radcliffe. A clear inspiration for the dramatic movement of the poem was, of course, *Romeo and Juliet*. Shakespeare is the "presider" over this poem to a larger extent than any other since the early passages of *Endymion*. Perhaps again his own love-passages had led Keats to "throw his whole being" into this play as he had done with *Troilus and Cressida* a few months before. The lovers in the poem play out their happier drama beset with the tremendous menace and danger of Shakespeare's warring families; "a hundred swords" are ready to put an end to their romance at the slightest false move. Old Angela the Beldam, who befriends the lovers, had much more of the character of Juliet's Nurse in Keats's own intended version of her speeches, before his publishers, careful to avoid religious as well as sexual offence in the poem, removed before publication some of her interjections of "Christ" and "Jesu." Moreover the story leaps from point to point in an entirely dramatic and Shakespearian way; even the climate points the drama, as Shakespeare's tempest does in *King Lear's* storm-scenes, which moved Keats so deeply. The frozen chill of the opening, the glowing warmth of the middle love-section, the wild and perilous storm of the ending, all make a dramatic sequence that develops with the actions of the characters in the story.

Yet the predominate feeling in *The Eve of St. Agnes* is not entirely literary, a piece of story-telling, nor merely dramatic, a play in stanza form. It is tangible, physical, and, above all, highly-colored and pictorial. Keats used pictorial terms himself about the poem when, talking of his plans for future works, he wrote, "I wish to diffuse the colouring of St Agnes eve throughout a Poem," and he speaks of its "drapery." One reason why the poem seems like a series of medieval pictures, giving a fresh view of the same story from stanza to stanza, like some jeweled fresco from a church wall, is that Keats had literally such a series in mind. It was the fruit of his own creative imagination working on the black-and-white prints he had seen three weeks before at Haydon's. His remark on these—"I do not think I ever had a greater treat out of Shake-speare"—was not a casual exaggeration, but had the weight of fact. Next to *Romeo and Juliet,* the chief dramatic motif of the poem is provided by the Campo Santo frescoes. Keats went on to describe them as "Full of Romance and the most tender feeling—magnifi-cence of draperies beyond any I ever saw." Already, in Haydon's studio, his eye was creating the color of a poem, the "drapery" of *St. Agnes.* It is easy to see which of the frescoes had this great effect on him. Keats's general description, "Specimens of the first and second age of art in Italy" is accurate in that there are two sets, a fifteenth-century Biblical sequence by Benozzo Gozzoli, and a more primitive fourteenth-century series. Keats's further remarks are significant:

> But Grotesque to a curious pitch—yet still making up a fine whole—even finer to me than more accomplish'd works—as there was left so much room for Imagination.

These make it certain that he is not referring to the far more fin-ished and elaborate Gozzoli frescoes of the Old Testament, which have the brilliance and sophistication of that artist's famous *Jour-ney of the Magi* at Florence. Keats's imagination had been stirred by the Primitives, and the way he commended them showed how great the effect had been. They were grotesque; that was, for him ever since childhood, a term of admiration, a sure way of arousing his interest. They "left so much room for Imagination" that they were the proper and almost inevitable material for poetry. More-over, though he did not perhaps know, one in particular of these primitives was a masterpiece of its kind, one of the most individual paintings in the world.

This was *The Triumph of Death* by an unknown master of the mid-fourteenth century. The fresco is in two halves, the left dra-matic and vivid. A medieval hunting-party of lords, ladies and grooms is suddenly confronted by the reminder of the grim physical facts of death; three corpses burst out of their coffins in horrible detail, one bloated, one decayed, one fleshless. Horror is dramati-cally conveyed by the faces and gestures of the party. The right-hand part of the fresco is a group of lovers, at court, with musical instruments. Yet even here is horror; devils swoop about their heads conveying lost souls to hell while angels try ineffectively to save them. The moral is pointed out by a series of composite pictures of the lives of hermits, one of whom leaves his cell to show these appalling sights to the revellers, and present to the hunting party a scroll reminding them that even in the pride of life man must die. Though the idea that in the midst of life we are in death is a common medieval pictorial conception there is an urgency and reality about this example that makes it far from a formal traditional exercise. It is, in historical fact, a terrible and accurate reflection of its own time, painted by someone who, as an adult, had actually experienced the Black Death, the most horrible plague to sweep across Europe. This is a picture of that time by a survivor, and its corpses that burst reeking from their coffins distorted by disease are no parable but the substances of death.

Keats had just come from a death-bed "of the most distressing nature"; his whole being for the rest of his days was suffused by this fact. Love, for him, never evades the background of death. This was why he bodied out the engraving of *The Triumph of Death* into the moving stanzas of a narrative poem in which the sense of death is ever-present. The sombre figure of the Beadsman, who begins and ends *The Eve of St. Agnes*, is the pervading hermit of *The Triumph of Death*, who is shown, like the Beadsman, praying with his rosary in his little austere chapel, setting the whole tone of the poem from the first stanza:

> St. Agnes' Eve—Ah, bitter chill it was!
> The owl, for all his feathers, was a-cold;
> The hare limp'd trembling through the frozen grass,
> And silent was the flock in woolly fold:
> Numb were the Beadsman's fingers, while he told
> His rosary, and while his frosted breath,
> Like pious incense from a censer old,
> Seem'd taking flight for heaven, without a death,
> Past the sweet Virgin's picture, while his prayer he saith. ˙

In the fresco, even the small detail of the hare is shown, crouching with other animals near the little door of the Beadsman's chapel, in the focal center of the engraving that Keats saw. The revelry of the poem in the midst of the icy chill of death that seems to encompass it, the literal picture

> Amid the timbrels, and the throng'd resort
> Of whisperers in anger or in sport;

is taken from the right-hand panel of the fresco, the gossiping court-
iers with instruments in their hands, oblivious of the destruction
just above their heads. The tragic and sinister end of the poem is
full of the atmosphere of the dramatic left-hand panel.

> And they are gone: ay, ages long ago
> These lovers fled away into the storm.
> That night the Baron dreamt of many a woe,
> And all his warrior-guests, with shade and form
> Of witch, and demon, and large coffin-worm,
> Were long be-nightmar'd. Angela the old
> Died palsy-twitch'd, with meagre face deform;
> The Beadsman, after thousand aves told,
> For aye unsought for slept among his ashes cold.

In the nightmare experience of the hunting-guests, large worms
crawl out of the bursting coffins before their eyes, plain even in the
uncolored engraving, while the ever-present demons wait close by
to snatch the living to a like horror. This aspect of Keats's poem
shows one of the most extraordinary and genuine cross-fertilizations
of one artist and one medium by another; the unknown fourteenth-
century painter and the Romantic poet are joined by chance in a
common realization of actual death, and the underlying reality and
full physical quality of the poem is the result.

The contrast between love and death had been the actual experience of Keats's childhood and adolescence. It was brought back
to him now by Tom's death, and he reverted to the love-dreams of
his own early days. As a schoolboy, dreaming of women, he said
"my mind was a soft nest in which some one of them slept though
she knew it not." Madeline, "trembling in her soft and chilly nest"
was an extension of this adolescent day-dream, her discovery while
sleeping a further version of the Chattertonian fragment about a
sleeping beauty attributed to Keats in his student days. Yet now,
his own tumultuous and mixed sexual feelings brought a need for
adult reality in the love theme of the poem. He later revised some
verses to show that the love-affair between Porphyro and Madeline
was physically consummated. Even the most explicit alteration,

> See while she speaks his arms encroaching slow
> Have zon'd her, heart to heart

seemed mild enough, though it nearly pushed Taylor out of publishing the whole poem, but Keats felt it vehemently and personally. He would despise, he said "a man who would be such an eunuch in sentiment as to leave a maid, with that Character about her, in such a situation." [3] With the death of Tom had died the last vestige of the hazy mock-Elizabethan common language they had about women; and though Madeline, "so pure a thing, so free from mortal taint," is not in the least like the women Keats had been meeting, imperial, enigmatic or flirtatious, they had aroused in him an underlying sexuality that pervades the whole poem.

Still, for all the adult realism behind it, the poem succeeds in capturing an energy of youth that goes back to the earliest springs of his poetry, released once more by Tom's death. In it, he drew on every experiment in poetry he had made since his initial Spenserian stanzas. It was, of course, his first lengthy attempt in that stanza, to which the poem owed a freedom that had never before appeared in his narratives, and it reached back to his apprentice reading, just as details reached back to his newly-awakened boyhood memories: as he told Clarke, the sounds of distant music that come and go throughout the poem were suggested by the sounds heard by himself and Holmes from the Headmaster's house at school. Besides Spenser, the eighteenth-century Spenserians he had just reread, even though he now condemned them, Tighe, Beattie and others, played their part. *The Minstrel* of the latter poet contributed to the new poem many echoes, and even one character, the Beldam —the same word used by both Beattie and Keats—who in both poems instructs the young hero in traditional superstition and folk-lore. Even a memory of poor Felton Mathew's verse helped the advent of the lovers' storm.[4] Keats's recent return to Chatterton

[3] Hyder Rollins, ed., *The Keats Circle*, I, 92.
[4] Compare:

> Hark! 'tis an elfin storm from faery land   (*The Eve of St. Agnes*, l. 343)

and

> Against the casement dark   (l. 324, draft)

with Mathew's

> Mark! while the squally wind and torrent rain
> Against the rattling casement   (*The Garland*, p. 154, Finney photostat)

was also present, though he rejected the more Chattertonian stanzas, to the poem's final benefit. Yet the technical tour-de-force of the poem is that it applies to all these early and essential groundworks of Keats's verse the recent hard labor and thought he had put into *Hyperion*. *The Eve of St. Agnes* is a poem where all this massive interplay of vowel and consonant finds a free unhampered narrative movement. It did not come easily, as his scored manuscript showed; this was not evidence of weakness in composition, but of the higher standards he was now applying to his poetry. Again and again, he begins a stanza with an idea or expression which would have seemed adequate to him six months before in *Isabella*, only to reject it, and try perhaps half-a-dozen radical variations before he is satisfied. The beautiful line "A chain-droop'd lamp was flickering by each door' appeared in no less than five different versions before the adjective "chain-droop'd" gave him the exact picture he wanted. *The Eve of St. Agnes* is the first and perhaps greatest fruit of his determination not to produce any more slipshod work for the critics; it is the most striking result of the application of his "own domestic criticism." The final impression of this poem, when all the elements of suggestion, local impression, artistic and literary influence have been assimilated, is that it is the first poem in which Keats speaks sustainedly and at full length in a voice entirely his, and in a medium over which he has complete and ample control.

Accident and chance played their part, of course, on a mind in which everything was absorbed into the web of creative agitation. On Saturday 23 January, Keats and Brown took leave of their elderly hosts in Eastgate Square, Chichester, and walked along the gusty exhilarating coast road to the waterside millhouse down by the harbor, thirteen miles away at Bedhampton. A letter wildly punning on the first syllable of the village told the Hampstead Dilkes of their arrival at the Snook house. There was also a postscript for "Millamant"—Fanny Brawne, from whom Keats had perhaps received a letter at Chichester.[5] In the same light-hearted mood in which the weekend had been passed, Keats and Brown went on an expedition on Monday 25 January to the dedication of Stansted Chapel. This was a great local event. The owner of the chapel and the estate of Stansted was Lewis Way, a rich man who

---

[5] *Letters*, II, 137, suggests this, though the sense is obscure.

had made his life work the conversion of the Jews. Ribald stories
were told of his Jewish guests at Stansted, where he hoped, unsuc-
cessfully, to found a College for them; more seriously, he had actually persuaded the Powers at Aix-la-Chapelle in 1818 to add a
clause to their protocol promising tolerance to the Jewish race.[6]
Way had chosen the Feast of the Conversion of St. Paul, 25 January, for the dedication of the building which he had raised from a
former hunting-lodge to a house of religion that bore the marks of
his own extremely individual character. The Regency Gothic design was of great delicacy. The owner's taste showed everywhere,
from the stained glass of the triple-arched windows in the nave,
embellished with scutcheons of the Fitzalan family, to the unique
painted East window, the only window in a Christian place of
worship that is wholly Jewish in design and symbolism. Texts
everywhere pointed to conversion and baptism, and as Way's own
daughter put it, "The idea throughout is the Gospel Dispensation
shadowed forth in the Law, or 'Moses a schoolmaster leading to
Christ.' "

Keats certainly did not go for religious reasons; but as he sat
through the long service with Brown and John Snook's small son
and namesake, he absorbed yet another version of the Gothic which
added to the crowded scene-painting of his poem. The triple windows, the rosy shields, the diamond panes and the colored light
shining on the congregation helped to make a picture transmuted
by the silver moonlight drench of imagination into

> A casement high and triple-arch'd there was,
> All garlanded with carven imag'ries
> Of fruits, and flowers, and bunches of knot-grass,
> And diamonded with panes of quaint device,
> Innumerable of stains and splendid dyes,
> As are the tiger-moth's deep-damask'd wings;
> And in the midst, 'mong thousand heraldries,
> And twilight saints, and dim emblazonings,
> A shielded scutcheon blush'd with blood of queens and kings.

Magnificent carvings by Grinling Gibbons, their motifs repeated
in the Chapel, were seen afterward in the house, which was thrown

---

[6] Bodleian MSS Eng. Lett. c. 139, f. 38.

open to the public, and which contained, again, in the words of
Way's daughter, "the great tapestry rooms, the wainscotted saloon,
the oak room with its fine paneling." Just as Keats was equally
affected and inspired by the genuine archaisms of Spenser and the
fake Middle English of Chatterton, so the medieval Gothic of Chichester and the Regency Gothic of Stansted fused in the setting of
his poem, where, it has been noticed, properties of a much later
date insinuate themselves into the bleak historical realism of the
opening. In the pressure of composition, every impression was
swept in, and it took the publishers' cautious proof-correction to
remove the hero's expletive "By the great St. Paul!" which signposts
the Stansted visit, and its new impetus to the poem.

Keats was lucky in every small detail of composition during this
poem. Brown, stimulating but distracting, left, the day after their
Stansted visit, for Wentworth Place. Keats's sore throat returned,
so he was not tempted by walks over the Downs, and did not go
past the garden gate. His hosts were quiet, homely and friendly,
not intellectuals; he had mild discussions on religion and politics
with the miller, who kindly promised to put on paper some of his
experience in farming to help George in America. Moreover, the
large thin blue sheets of paper Haslam had found, so that they
would fold in a small packet for his own letters to George, proved
to be ideal for the composition of a poem where there was a lot of
crossing-out and marginal alteration. The poem had its difficulties
and hesitations mainly at strongly human moments. Keats found
it hard to undress his heroine convincingly in front of the concealed Porphyro, and the consummation of their love dissatisfied
him so much that he afterwards tried to make it more explicit;
yet it is a mark of his new poetic conscience that just those places
eventually show his master-strokes. The touch in Madeline's disrobing

Unclasps her warmed jewels one by one

has been picked out for praise by many later critics; it is typical
of the care he now gave to every small turn that the slack original
"bosom jewels" was rejected from a poem that never once loses
its grip. . . .

The Dangers of Enthrallment

by Clifford Adelman

There is a very thin line between the dream and the waking world. There is a very thin line between sensations and what Keats called "high sensations." [1] Yet on this thin line lie the uncertainties which characterize the human situation. As Wordsworth, Goethe, and other Romantics also implied, the border is, in fact, the human situation. Souls cannot be made in a world of certainties. There is no urgency there. Souls must be made, says Keats, in a world where "axioms in philosophy are not axioms until they are proved upon our pulse" [2]; and the starting point for the proof is that of uncertainty. We are in mists, Keats says in the sonnet written on top of Ben Nevis, and "even such, / Even so vague is man's sight of himself!" The traveler know only "that all my eye doth meet / Is mist and Crag, . . . not only on this height / But in the world of thought and mental might." The poetical character, then, must remain in uncertainty, for only in suspension and flight can it explore and create. To find a resting place, a peak from which to observe and nod, like Wordsworth, is not to create; nor can one fall off that thin line into the certainties of sensations or thoughts. To do so, for Keats, is to become enthralled, and one cannot create from enthrallment.

Keats himself never used the term, "enthrallment," but there is a good deal of justification for our so doing. Keats does come close: the "Pale warriors" of the knight's dream in "La Belle Dame sans Merci" awaken his thinking principle with the "horrid warning,"

"The Dangers of Enthrallment" by Clifford Adelman. *An original essay printed here for the first time. Excerpted and revised from an unpublished monograph,* *"Keats's Concept of the Dream and its Function."*

[1] *The Letters of John Keats,* ed. M. B. Forman, London, 1960, p. 139.

[2] *Ibid.,* p. 141.

" 'La Belle Dame sans Merci / Hath thee in thrall!' " And in Keats'
letter to John Hamilton Reynolds of May 3, 1818, in which he
presents his elaborate analogy of "human life to a large Mansion
of Many Apartments," the *concept* of enthrallment first arises:
"the awakening of this thinking principle within us" marks the
passage from the "thoughtless Chamber" to the "Chamber of
Maiden-Thought," but

> . . . we no sooner get into the second Chamber . . . than we become
> intoxicated with the light and the atmosphere, we see nothing but
> pleasant wonders, and think of delaying there for ever in delight. . . .[3]

If the discovery of truth lies in making ourselves Souls, and if
this discovery takes place in an uncertain realm in which our imaginative speculations are the means by which we *continually* die into
life, then the discovery is both processional and necessary. Enthrallment, on the other hand, prevents us from making ourselves Souls.
It freezes our progress, either on the borderland, or in one of the
Chambers. It binds us to a world of certainties, to what Blake
called "one-fold vision."

The experience of the knight in "La Belle Dame sans Merci"
most adequately testifies to the dangers of enthrallment. Like
Adam, the knight of "La Belle Dame sans Merci" wakes to find his
dream true. He dreams of a sensory death, and awakes to a spiritual one with its objective correlatives, "the cold hill's side," the
withered sedge, the funeral flowers which wreath his pale brow.
The knight, of course, thought he was dreaming about something
else, something far more delightful, and it took the dream-within-a-
dream to awaken him, to disengage him from his enchantment.
The elfin lady's enchantment was no ordinary medieval love spell.
It was something far more sinister (otherwise the "warning" would
not be so terrifying)—she had him "in thrall." But one enthrallment leads to another: enchanted by both mystery and delight in
the meads, the knight dreams of death (his own spiritual stasis),
and when we find him awake on the cold hill's side, he is enthralled
again, loitering in the languor of a death-wish.

The man enthralled is he who remains trapped in one of the

---

[3] *Ibid.*, p. 142. These are the only two Chambers which Keats claims he can
describe, "the doors of the rest being as yet shut upon me."

Chambers of the mind whose attitude toward conventions, beliefs, and the language which expresses them remains static. Such a man remains, in effect, in an unauthentic dream: he never wakes up, never finds his dream true, and thus never truly becomes a Soul. To awaken from the dream is to awaken from enthrallment, to pass from one Chamber to another. In order to objectify and overcome his own susceptibility to enthrallment, Keats attempted to dramatize the problems and dangers of that state in three major poems between the autumn of 1817 and the spring of 1819: "La Belle Dame sans Merci," "Ode to a Nightingale," and "The Eve of St. Agnes." In so doing, he himself made a significant advance from the Chamber of Maiden-Thought.

"The Eve of St. Agnes," despite the rapidity of composition and a seemingly gossamer subject, is the most elaborate of these objectifications. Its dramatic structure enables us to watch the effects of various modes and degrees of enthrallment, whether within the context of the dream-awakening passage of Porphyro and Madeline, or in the contrasting contexts of Angela, the beadsman, and the revellers. Every character in this poem is enthralled in some way— every character except the narrator, that is. For it is his metaphorical dramaturgy which enables him to attain the aesthetic distance of negative capability, the distance necessary to distinguish reality principle from enthrallment, the authentic from the unauthentic.

The beadsman comes to us in the first stanza, with a heavy sense of the immediacy of the phenomenal world. The images are stark, direct, and wholly sensory. They create the sense of a pervasive cold, a chill which intensifies through the qualifiers until capped by the "numb" of the beadsman's fingers. Naïvely the old man equates his visible "frosted breath" with a heaven-bound soul, and pities "the sculptur'd dead" who "seem to freeze." They are, of course, the frozen, or fixed, images of once-living knights and ladies. To the beadsman, they are also frozen by the cold. The beadsman, for all his humanizing sympathy vis-à-vis the statues has, in Wallace Stevens' term, "a mind of winter," a mind tied to phenomena.

But we wonder: a man such as the beadsman, involved in religious orthodoxies, must believe in two worlds. However, it would seem that his religiosity has been inherited, not discovered; accepted, not questioned, and hence lifeless, dependent on both ritual and icon; that his sympathy is thus for the dead, not for the living, and that even his sympathy for the dead is motivated by dogmatic prescription, and not by any human qualities of the dead.

The beadsman is thus enthralled: he feels no tension between his *Lebensform* and those of the world about him. He does not see beyond his own chamber, down the various passageways which lead away from it. In fact, in a manner prefigurative of all the other enthralled characters in the poem, he has assimilated all that is foreign to him by qualifying it in the language which he understands best. To be sure, we all have a tendency to do just that; but the man of negative capability does not—and he makes himself a Soul. The two worlds *are* there about the beadsman, but the only connection he can make between them is the connection of the icon, the phenomenal symbol through which he is able to realize and empathize with the metaphysical world. But the icon is reductive and static; and the metaphysical world with which the beadsman empathizes is a world of death. We are not very surprised, then, to find him dead—numbed, frozen—sleeping among his ashes in stanza XLII. In a metaphorical sense, that's just where Keats left him in the third stanza: enthralled, static, sleeping, dead.

In the third and fourth stanzas of the poem, we first become aware of other chambers, of other modes of sound and color, of other ways of life. "Music's golden tongue" enters from a yet unseen room. This first intrusion of another reality, a suggestion, a half-hint, is quickly withdrawn. In the fourth stanza, the beadsman hears "the prelude soft," that is, receives another indirect hint of the reality in the surrounding chambers; and by "prelude," a hint of the intensification of that reality to come. Another, and one of the most important, details in Keats' preparation for the presentation of the other major actors in the poem is the image of the carved angels on the hammer-beams of the castle hall. "Carved angels" and "sculptured dead" belong, respectively, to the worlds of the revellers and the beadsman. They are fixed images, and thus, perhaps, an adequate objective correlative to the enthrallment of those characters fixed outside the realm of the Porphyro-Madeline drama. The fact that Madeline becomes a *living* angel, so to speak, in stanza XXV, suggests the contrast; and the reference to Porphyro

as "pale as smooth-sculptured stone" (297) during the transformation scene also reacts back on these initial images to give them
additional weight.

I stress these carvings in wood and stone because, as I hope to
demonstrate, Porphyro's and Madeline's consciousness of the existence and value of different levels of reality is wrought, not through
the use of conventional representations or icons such as those on
which the castle rests, or those which the beadsman values, but
through the living experience of the dream. Such an experience
is opposed both to the reductive rigidity of the icon, and to the
passive and unthinking acceptance of conventions.

> upon St. Agnes' Eve
> Young virgins *might have* visions of delight,
> And soft adorings from their loves receive
> Upon the honey'd middle of the night,
> *If* ceremonies due they did aright;
> As, supperless to bed they *must* retire,
> And couch supine their beauties, lily white;
> Nor look behind, nor sideways, but require
> Of Heaven with upward eyes for all that they desire.
>
> (46–54; italics mine)

There are many possible dispositions with which one can approach any convention or belief. And each disposition, in effect,
declares the belief or convention to possess a certain authenticity
and value—at least for the believer. But Keats believed that such
authenticity and value must be discovered, not accepted. Nothing
is real or true until it is "proved upon our pulses." In Madeline's
case, the value of the prescribed conventions and beliefs of St.
Agnes' Eve remains indeterminate until she awakens from her
enthrallment with the ritual. Of course, as was the case of the
knight in "La Belle Dame sans Merci," it is possible to move from
one enthrallment to another, but in this drama that danger is confronted, experienced, and overcome by both Madeline and Porphyro.

As we first see Madeline, she is dancing through the crowded,
noisy hall of the revellers in a trance. She sees only cloaks, not
bodies or faces. She is so enthralled with St. Agnes' prescriptions
that she is gradually extinguishing all her sensory responses: "She
scarcely heard . . . she saw not . . ." (57, 62). Anticipating "Agnes'

dreams" (63), she has moved into the penumbra of the waking world. The implication is that the chamber of the revellers is wholly a sensory world which can be apprehended only sensorially. By abandoning one mode of apprehension for another, Madeline is looking toward another chamber. Her present existence in the chamber of the revellers is thus a borderline one.

She appears to be "Hoodwink'd with faery fancy" (70). Ironic readings of the poem claim, in effect, that Madeline is thus hoodwinked throughout. But the "faery fancy," by the dramatic terms of the poem, has an indeterminate value at this point; and we err if we extend the perceptual judgment of Madeline's initial situation in the chamber of the revellers to her entire experience in the poem. If we read Madeline as merely the deceived and seduced maid, then we ourselves are enthralled. All we can claim at this point is that there is something wrong with the *Lebensform* of the revellers (the narrator has dismissed them offhandedly—"These let us wish away" [41]), and that Madeline is set apart from them (though such spatial relations do not necessarily imply that there's anything "right" with her), and that she is walking around "amort" (70), in a trance, a trance which may be a simple deception or a more serious enthrallment.

In any case, Keats carries Madeline over into the ninth stanza, where he introduces Porphyro. The object of the juxtaposition is more than dramatic. Madeline, "purposing each moment to retire, . . . linger'd still" (73–4) in the "glowing" (33) chamber of the revellers, while Porphyro stands "Beside the portal doors, / Buttress'd from moonlight . . ." (76–7). Both are beyond the reach of the silvery moonlight—Porphyro in darkness, Madeline in the light of the great hall.

Again, and at this moment, we can say little about the significance of the moonlight, but we can say something about the other modes of light. Both the darkness which conceals Porphyro and the light of the great hall belong to the physical world. We have seen the darkness before in the color scheme associated with the beadsman's world, a world of "sculptur'd dead," a world of nonfulfillment. The artificial light of the chambers is associated with the insubstantial and meaningless gestures and lives of the revellers who move through them.

Now in one sense Porphyro is, at this moment, moving very much in that physical, waking world. He has come to the castle with a design in mind, and is confronted with a very dangerous situation. At the same time, however, he is propelled by a force which does not heed the clear and present dangers. Only one totally enthralled, as enchanted by expectation as is Madeline, one who thinks of his heart as a "citadel" (84), would be mad enough to enter the castle of his enemies. Enthrallment in this hostile world can literally lead to death.

In Porphyro's case, the enthrallment also leads to a distorted vision of Angela. After she leads him to the first of the moonlit chambers in which he will find himself, he conjures her as if she were herself involved in romance occultism:

> "O tell me, Angela, by the holy loom
> Which none but secret sisterhood may see,
> When they St. Agnes' wool are weaving piously." (114–16)

When Angela first appears, she is "Shuffling along with ivory-headed wand." (92) Keats first wrote "staff" instead of "wand," and the shift is wholly in keeping with Porphyro's enchanted vision of Angela as he looks at her "Like a puzzled urchin on an aged crone / Who keepeth clos'd a wond'rous riddle-book" (129–30), and swears by the saints and prayers of the very ritual in which Madeline is enthralled.

But Angela keeps no secrets. Her sensibilities, tied to the concrete, to the harsh world of the hall downstairs and the storm outside, enable her to think only in literal terms. She operates in this drama as an agent conscious of her very realistic part in helping Porphyro intensify the deception of Madeline. It is she who interprets his "stratagem" strictly in terms of cold human motivation and desire. To be sure, something sexual does eventually go in the chamber, but it is transformed by Porphyro and Madeline even beyond the world of mere romance in which both of them enter the poem. It is not merely a question of a seduction *per se*—the only way Angela can conceive of it—but of how one values what goes on in the chamber: is it something banal? tinged by romance? something visionary and transforming? or something else? Precisely because Angela is so tied to the mundane, so enthralled in the

literal, she meets her end in the harshest qualifiers drawn from
that sensory world which is both her mode of conceptualization and
her stage:

> Angela the old
> Died palsy-twitch'd, with meagre face deform. (375–)

It is a case of metaphoric justice. Like the beadsman, she dies in
her chamber of enthrallment.

Nonetheless, Angela inadvertantly participates in the spiritual
drama of the two lovers. Because Porphyro is so enthralled in romance, Angela must lead him through the various halls of the
castle, must keep him out of danger and arrange his meeting with
Madeline. Porphyro's enthrallment in romance is an object of near-
mockery. Until he arrives in Madeline's chamber, Porphyro is
hardly self-propelled. Angela virtually drags him through the castle
to Madeline's closet. Even when he protests Angela's interpretation
of his "stratagem," he does so as one still in the thoughtless chamber, with the overstatement and braggadocio of the language in
which he is enthralled:

> "I will not harm her, by all saints I swear,"
> Quoth Porphyro: "O may I ne'er find grace
> When my weak voice shall whisper its last prayer,
> If one of her soft ringlets I displace,
> Or look with ruffian passion in her face:
> Good Angela, believe me by these tears;
> Or I will, even in a moment's space,
> Awake, with horrid shout, my foremen's ears,
> And beard them, though they be more fang'd than wolves and bears."
>
> (145–53)

Porphyro, like Madeline in her enchantment, is described as "cold"
(134) or "pale" (169) because his enthrallment stifles motion and
fulfillment. Even if we were to interpret Porphyro's original plan
on the same crass plane as does Angela, the diction of romance in
which he describes that plan precludes a mere seduction; he hopes
to

> win perhaps that night a peerless bride,
> While legion'd fairies pac'd the coverlet,

And pale enchantment held her sleepy-eyed.
Never on such a night have lovers met,
Since Merlin paid his Demon all the monstrous debt. (167–71)

The reference to Merlin is a narrative judgment on Porphyro's present state of mind. Merlin, in effect, "hoodwinked" himself, became enthralled to such a degree that he was trapped by his own magic. As long as Porphyro allows his language to distort reality, as long as he is unconscious of the value or authenticity of the reality created by his language, he runs the same risk, in this castle, as did Merlin within his hollow oak. Porphyro's metaphorical task in the poem is to awaken to the value and authenticity of his dream, and thus to pass out of the chamber in which he is enthralled.

Having positioned Porphyro in Madeline's room by the guiding hand of Angela, having readied the feast, Keats has to move Madeline herself upstairs. But in order to remind us what sort of a state Madeline is in, he interjects stanza XXII, in which Madeline, now totally entranced, instinctively and almost unconsciously helps Angela get downstairs. The geographical separation is significant: Angela returns to the literal world—the lower chambers and the great hall—and the upper world of potential vision is cut off from it for the rest of the poem.

But that separation is not complete until all tokens or signs of the lower chambers have been extinguished. Here, that other detail of stanza XXII—that Madeline still carries a silver taper—takes on additional weight when Keats emphasizes the sudden extinguishing of that light in the next stanza: "Out went the taper as she hurried in; / Its little smoke, in pallid moonshine, died" (199–200). It is as if Madeline's room itself extinguishes the light brought from those other and alien halls below. A more natural light, the "pallid moonshine," seems to enter in order to preside over the ensuing events.

Madeline, however, is not conscious of the moonlight, the source of which lies outside the castle. She is as yet unfulfilled in her hopes of vision, even though she is "all akin / To spirits of the air, and visions wide" (201–202). She is still a "tongueless nightingale" (206). At this moment, any potential vision would "die, heart-stifled, in her dell" (207), precisely because her enthrallment is so intense as to render her oblivious to the world outside, oblivious to the spirit which, under the aegis of the moonlight, begins to fill the room.

What is the nature of this more-informing spirit of which both Porphyro and Madeline are to become conscious? It is revealed in Keats' description of the chamber: we have "carven imag'ries" (209) which are seemingly akin to the "sculptur'd dead" of the beadsman or the "carved angels" on which the cornices of the castle rest. But the sculptures of Madeline's chamber are composed of organic images: "fruits, and flowers, and bunches of knot-grass" (210). The process of engrafting the organic on the lifeless is carried on first by plants, then by the colors of the glass panes through which the pallid moonlight is transformed, and finally by human symbolic expressions: the "shielded scutcheon blush'd with blood of queens and kings" (206).

The cornerstone of this description is the metaphor of potential transformation. Neither the beadsman, nor Angela, nor the revellers, in their literalism or enthrallment in various thoughtless chambers, are concerned with any other possible level of reality or value. But as the silver light of a heavenly vision shines through the window, it is mediated by the highly vitalistic images and colors on the panes, so that Madeline, kneeling in this light, appears to be "a splendid angel" (223). The combination of religiosity and romance, of the visionary and the earthly ideal, mirrored in the merging of the color scheme, looks forward to the kind of transforming realization which will liberate Madeline from her enchantment.

And through all Keats' revisions in the next stanza (XXVI), his verbals remain constant: "Unclasps," and "Loosens," to which is added, in the final version, "frees." All these verbs suggest liberation. Indeed the "awakening of the thinking principle" toward which Madeline is being drawn, unconsciously, by imperceptible degrees, involves suggestion or implication rather than delineation.

But like the intrusion of "Music's golden tongue" (20) into the world of the beadsman, the suggestion of Madeline's movement away from the enthrallment which has rendered her speechless is quickly withdrawn. Madeline is still "Half-hidden" (231), still unfulfilled. She "dreams awake, and sees, / In fancy" (232–3), and what she sees is consequently an abstraction, not a reality, a moonlit

image of her enthrallment, unmediated by the organic color scheme
of the world into which one wakes to discover whether dreams
are true or not. That her present state is a kind of borderland on
the way to the awakening is indicated by the narrator's own vague-
ness of diction in stanza XXVII when he speaks of Madeline in a
"sort of wakeful swoon" (236).

The perjorative aspects of this swoon are indicated by the movement of the narrator's analogies through the rest of the stanza.
By speaking of the "poppied warmth of sleep" (237), Keats implies
that Madeline's state is akin to that of the drugged, and hence, un-
natural. Madeline's soul is also "Flown, like a thought, until the
morrow-day" (239). That which is supposedly the center of her
being, her soul, is, in a state of enthrallment, a trifle. Souls cannot
be made in such a state; identities cannot be discovered; and one
can never wake from such dreams to find them true. That Keats
is moving toward a statement of negative value concerning Madeline's present condition becomes quite apparent in the shift from
"haven'd" (240) to "Blinded" (242). The parallel construction of
the sentences supports and draws our attention to this shift:

> Blissfuly haven'd both from joy and pain (240)

> Blinded alike from sunshine and from rain (242)

What first appears to be a statement concerning Madeline's invulnerability becomes something sinister, finally to change from
threat to promise in the concluding simile: "As though a rose
should shut, and be a bud again" (243).

The progression of the metaphor is now clear. We move from
invulnerability to blindness to potential (the bud). The closing or
regression of the rose thus becomes a necessary stage on the road
to its further and fuller blooming. And by employing the vehicles
of the organic bud and rose, Keats implies that the opening of
the bud is a gesture "imperceptibly impelled"—like the awakening
of the thinking principle, for instance.

When Porphyro emerges from his hiding, and the two lovers are
spatially established as distinct though adjacent, the two dominant
image patterns of the poem come to reinforce the situation. The
light-color pattern is present in the contrast of the "dim, silver

twilight" (252) and the "cloth of woven crimson, gold, and jet" (254). And sound images, which had previously taken the opposing forms of the beadsman's "dumb oratories," "frosted breath," and recitations, and the instrumental music of the revellers, reappear in "The boisterous, midnight, festive clarion" (258) which "affrays" Porphyro's ears—"affray" being tonally consistent with the way in which Keats originally qualified the revellers' music: "The silver, snarling trumpets 'gan to chide" (31). The significance of this momentary intrusion of the world of the revellers is two-fold: first, it keeps both Porphyro and the reader conscious of the presence of the other chambers, chambers through which both have already travelled (though the significance of that process has yet to be realized); secondly, the music downstairs is wholly instrumental, music which relies very much on something beyond the self for its existence.

Keats is not playing with such contrasts to display his talents in creating patterns of imagery. There is a subtle and metaphorical dialectic operating in those patterns. In stanza XXXIII, Porphyro takes up the lute and sings. Song, the synthesis of language and music, has been absent from the catalogue of aural images presented thus far. The gray world of the beadsman only speaks, and even then its speech is "dumb." The golden unthinking world of the revellers is too noisy. In fact, that world is filled with mere noise, not music, not harmony; and by its reliance on instruments, the world of the revellers reveals its neglect of the human capacity to create and harmonize in song. And song embraces language, the medium of communication, apprehension, and awareness among human beings, the medium by which the truth of our dreams is expressed. Without verbal expression, we remain enthralled in our dreams.

Indeed, when Porphyro picks up the lute in stanza XXXIII, the narrator speaks of him as "Awakening" (289). The use of the word is varied, as the narrator seems to speak indiscriminately of both Porphyro and Madeline as "awake." After Keats finally gets Madeline undressed, she "dreams awake, and sees, / In fancy . . ." (232–3). Then she lies in "sort of wakeful swoon" (236), but a dangerous one: "poppied . . . oppress'd . . . fatigued . . ." (237–8). She is awake, but with no control over her faculties, having submitted to the ritual, and lies "Clasp'd like a missal" (241)—a phrase which recalls the monolithic commitment of the beadsman, and thus another psychologically unhealthy constraint. In stanza XXVIII, Porphyro infers that Madeline is asleep by the commencement of heavy, set breathing; but the narrator speaks of that commencement as an awakening:

> Porphyro gazed upon her empty dress,
> And listen'd to her breathing if it chanced
> To wake into a slumberous tenderness;
> Which when he heard, that minute did he bless,
> And breath'd himself . . . (245–9)

Waking to sleep is no paradox in the total context of Madeline's progress: it is really the beginning of the drama of her awakening. At the same time, Porphyro continues his plunge into enthrallment, so entranced with playing out the drama of the dream that he becomes its mindless slave. It is no wonder that Madeline awakes from one dream only to find another which she cannot accept.

There seems to be something highly artificial and fragile about the external trappings and language of romance, and certainly something false about the attempt to assert such trappings as anything more than the products of an enthralled fancy. Porphyro is constantly trying to make such an assertion. In dragging out all the "delicates," the fairy food of stanza XXX, so that they stand "sumptuous . . . / In the retired quiet of the night, / Filling the chilly room with perfume light . . ." (273–5), and simultaneously asking Madeline to awake as a "seraph fair" (276), he has tried to force the blending of actuality and romance. Madeline will recognize the fusion to be a false one, and will force that recognition back on Porphyro.

But when Porphyro first asks Madeline to awake (stanza XXXI), she is at the height of her enthrallment, frozen in the first chamber in a "midnight charm / Impossible to melt as iced stream . . ." (282–3). Awakenings cannot be forced—they are necessary, imperceptibly impelled. Furthermore, Madeline would never awaken to the call of one who is, at the moment, as frozen and invulnerable ("unnerved") as she. Porphyro cannot, therefore, penetrate her dream, even physically, without conscious consent, which is why he asks her so imploringly, "Open thine eyes" (278). He certainly cannot redeem her vision and transform it into something real. We cannot say that he is even aware of the redemptive value of the total experience in the chamber. The artificial colors, silver and gold, still frame the proceedings, and Porphyro's "phantasies" are as "woofed" (288) as the gorgeous tablecloth. He is thus never aware of the incongruity between his religio-romance diction and the fleshy surroundings and sensual overtones of his addresses. But Porphyro revives again in stanza XXXIII, and introduces song into the vision.

Even though he himself is reviving ("Awakening," in a sense) "an ancient ditty, long since mute," (291), Porphyro is not out of his own enthrallment. He is, after all, trying to force the song directly on Madeline's sensory apprehension, "Close to her ear touching the melody" (293), thus reverting, if temporarily, to the sensory world of Angela. And when Madeline first opens her eyes, Porphyro sinks to his knees, "pale as smooth-sculptured stone" (297)—a phrase which throws us back to the beadsman and his statues. Madeline wants the reality, not the icon, wants the living thing, spiritual and physical, and not the sign or abstraction, not merely the words.

If physicality is to enter Madeline's vision, if the dream, in the terms of Keats's Epistle to Reynolds, is to rescue the waking world from "shadows," it had better do so naturally, and not by false inducement. For such reasons does Madeline say that Porphyro is "pallid, chill, and drear" (311). He has assumed the traditional romance posture of the abject lover, or, alternatively, a sepulchric attitude reminiscent of the beadsman's chapel. Both recall abstract and hence cold beings, while Madeline wants a reality within her dream, wants the sensuality and voluptuousness which have appeared to both lovers only as images. Porphyro and Madeline, then, have been partially trapped in the same manner as the beadsman. The lovers have accepted the language and conventions of their respective "chambers." Because Porphyro and Madeline have, in their enthrallments, merely accepted the world of romance, they have not made any "axioms" true, and thus the language and conventions are not viable, not authentic.

But here Madeline asks Porphyro to stay, and, in effect, to seduce her, which, when done, proves to be a double awakening for her. For only after her dream has been realized in bed does it take on the "colours from the Sunset" which make it an authentic imaginative dream. By Keats' logic, Madeline thus awakens yet again, this time to find the dream true, and passes from her enthrallment into the consciousness of pain and suffering—and love—in the waking world.

Porphyro is on his knees, wan and pale and fairly loitering, and Madeline opens her eyes, *but* still sees the images of her dream—that is, for a moment she is unable to make the distinction between the dream and the reality. Porphyro was alive in her dream, corporeal. And her responses to him there were "pure and deep" (301). The "painful change" (300) in Porphyro's appearance results from a shift in Madeline's perspective. She awakens from enthrallment and the image of her lover to find kneeling down beside the bed not the reality of her dream but simply another icon. So she asks Porphyro to move from one false trance (his) into another (her dream), to vitalize the images of the dream and thus make them true. She asks him not to leave her on the borderland of the dream and the waking world, a land of uncertainties, doubts, and fears. She wants to be able to combine the best of both worlds while remaining in the dream. This is sheer delusion! When physicality enters the dream, mutability enters, and both Porphyro and Madeline must then pass out of the chamber of their respective fairy enthrallments: "St. Agnes' moon" (324) must set. In order to break the false enthrallment, the lovers cannot lock themselves in dream, but must actualize the visionary experience.

The action of the transformation, the rite of passage, is totally metaphorized through the blending of the color-image patterns. Sensuality is carried by vitalistic colors. At first "pallid, chill, and drear" (311), Porphyro now "arose, / Ethereal, flush'd, and like a throbbing star / Seen mid the sapphire heaven's deep repose" (317–19). It is not merely that the sensory rose is combined with the visionary star. Rather, the context in which Porphyro is moving has changed. The fact that he is "seen" as a star indicates that his being is a function of the disposition of the perceiver. Both the narrator and Madeline, if only for a moment, have seen him simultaneously exist in the world of the immortal dream and that of mutability.

Like all great Romantic surmises, the moment of pure intuition can occur only in a dash or a colon, a suspension of the world of words. The memory of the moment continues, of course, in the world of words—which is paradoxically why such intuition is immortal. But from omega we can only move to alpha, and back into the physical world the lovers go, with the frost and wind and setting moon. That Porphyro foresees the return (his own "change," though not so "painful") is evident in his use of the same language that the narrative voice employed to describe the initial moments of the falling action: "pattereth," "flaw-blown sleet" (324). With the sleet and pain, the two lovers, briefly blended in the moment when the sensory nature of the dream was realized and made true upon the pulses, are back in a world of division, confronted with a direct and explicit possibility of separation.

It is Madeline, of course, who looks at the situation from the point of view of division, being the maid seduced and fearful of being abandoned. Porphyro, on the other hand, is desirous of completing the union begun metaphorically in the dream, desirous of making the whole dream true—which, we might say, was his object all along though he did not realize it. It may seem strange that, after awakening, Porphyro seems to be trying to transform reality back into the dream, and using the medium of language to do so (he is a "vassal blest" [335], "a famish'd pilgrim,—saved by miracle" [339], and perhaps a "rude infidel" [342]; he refers to the tempest as "an elfin-storm from faery land" [43]). But at this point, passing out of the chamber of his enthrallment, Porphyro knows what he is talking about. He now has the ability to perceive differentially, and those words have significance and value—the passage from dream to waking has made them true. And Madeline hurries *"at his words,* beset with fears, / For there were sleeping dragons all around, / At glaring watch, perhaps, with ready spears" (352–4; italics mine). It is Porphyro's language which prompts her to act, though that language seems to come from their mutual experience in the dream, and the dream still colors (with "sleeping dragons") the world to which she awakes. Keats cannot follow the lovers beyond the castle gates and into the storm. But the lovers' language creates their certainty, and the storm, for them, becomes "an elfin-storm from faery land, / Of haggard seeming, but a boon indeed" (343–4). Porphyro and Madeline demonstrate, by the combination of highly practical actions necessary to escape from their worldly prison and the language of romance with which that escape is described, that they have found the border between the waking and dreaming worlds. So we really do not fear for them as they find a "darkling way" (355) through the castle and "glide, like phantoms" (361) through the great hall and into the night. We do not fear for them because their language now sustains the truth of the dream and because, in their elopement, they are proving the authenticity of the dream upon their pulses. They, the "phantoms," are truly awake, while the rest of the castle remains enthralled in a wholly sensory world.

Chronology of Important Dates

	Keats	The Age
1795	John Keats is born in London on October 31, eldest son of Thomas Keats, manager of a livery stable, and Frances Jennings. Subsequent children are George (1797–1841), Thomas (1799–1818), Edward (1801, dies in infancy), and Frances Mary, called Fanny (1803–89).	
1798		Wordsworth's and Coleridge's *Lyrical Ballads*.
1803–11	With George and, later, Tom, attends Clarke's school at Enfield, north of London.	
1804	His father dies in a fall from a horse in April. His mother remarries in June, and the children go to live with their grandparents.	Napoleon crowned Emperor
1807		Wordsworth's *Poems in Two Volumes*.
1808		Goethe's *Faust*, Part I.
1810	His mother dies of tuberculosis in March.	
1811–15	Apprenticeship to an apothecary-surgeon at Edmonton.	The Regency (1811–20).

1812		Byron's "Childe Harold," Cantos I and II.
1814	Writes earliest poems (beginning with "Imitation of Spenser.")	Wordsworth's "The Excursion."
1815	Enters Guy's Hospital, London, in October to begin further medical training.	Napoleon defeated at Waterloo.
1816	His first published poem (the sonnet "O Solitude!") appears in May. Passes apothecaries' examination in July. Accelerated poetic activity beginning in August.	Shelley's "Alastor"; Coleridge's "Christabel," "Kubla Khan," and "The Pains of Sleep"; Byron's "Childe Harold," Canto III.
1817	His first volume, *Poems*, published in March. Begins "Endymion" in April.	Coleridge's *Biographia Literaria* and *Sibylline Leaves*.
1818	Writes "Isabella" (February–April). "Endymion" published in April. George Keats and his bride emigrate to America in June. Walking tour through northern England and Scotland in June–August. Begins "Hyperion" in September. Meets Fanny Brawne. Tom Keats dies of tuberculosis in December.	Shelley's "The Revolt of Islam"; Byron's "Childe Harold," Canto IV
1819	Writes the poems that put him "among the English Poets": "The Eve of St. Agnes" (January–February), "La Belle Dame sans Merci" (April), the odes—"Psyche, "Nightingale," "Grecian Urn," "Melancholy" (April–May), "Lamia" and "The Fall of Hyperion" (July–September), "To Autumn" (September).	Byron's "Don Juan," Cantos I and II.

1820	Severe hemorrhage in the lungs in February (the final illness now under way). His third volume, *Lamia, Isabella, The Eve of St. Agnes, and Other Poems,* published in July. Sails for Italy in September.	Death of George III. Shelley's *Prometheus Unbound.*
1821	Dies in Rome on February 23.	Shelley's "Epipsychidion," and "Adonais."

Notes on the Editor and Contributors

ALLAN DANZIG, the editor, teaches at City College, New York. He has written articles about Romantic and Victorian poetry and about Vladimir Nabokov.

CLIFFORD ADELMAN teaches at City College, New York, and is currently working on a study of Keats's concept of the dream.

WALTER JACKSON BATE, Lowell Professor of the Humanities at Harvard, is known for his work in eighteenth century and Romantic literature. His books include *From Classic to Romantic, The Achievement of Samuel Johnson,* and some portions of *Criticism: The Major Texts.* In addition to his critical biography of Keats, he has written *Negative Capability* and *The Stylistic Development of Keats.*

BERNARD BLACKSTONE has written *English Blake, The Consecrated Urn,* and, most recently, *Virginia Woolf.*

ROBERT GITTINGS, poet and critic, preceded his biography of Keats with *The Mask of Keats* and *John Keats: The Living Year.*

JACK STILLINGER teaches at the University of Illinois. He has written several articles on Keats, and assisted Hyder Rollins in preparing the standard edition of Keats *Letters.* He has edited Wordsworth and the *Letters of Charles Brown,* and will shortly bring out an anthology of essays on Keats's poetry.

EARL WASSERMAN, Chairman of the English Department at The Johns Hopkins University, is the author of *Elizabethan Poetry in the Eighteenth Century, The Scholarly Origin of the Elizabethan Revival, Pope's Epistle to Bathurst,* and *The Subtler Language: Critical Readings of Neoclassic and Romantic Poems,* as well as many articles on eighteenth century and Romantic literature.

HERBERT G. WRIGHT is the author of *Boccaccio in England from Chaucer to Tennyson.* He has edited *Seventeenth Century Modernization of the First Three Books of Troilus and Criseyde.*

Selected Bibliography

Richard Fogel. *The Imagery of Keats and Shelley*. Hamden, Connecticut: Archon Books, 1962. Especially useful is Chapter Five, "Concrete and Abstract Imagery," in which he discusses "The Eve of St. Agnes."

Robert Gittings. *John Keats: The Living Year*. Cambridge, Massachusetts: Harvard University Press, 1954. Recounts in detail the development of the poem and the biographical influences in it.

Davis Perkins. *The Quest for Permanence*. Cambridge, Massachusetts: Harvard University Press, 1959. In the Chapter "The Uncertainties of Vision" discusses the nature of vision, dream, and poetry, and their relationship in the poem.

Aileen Ward. *John Keats: The Making of a Poet*. New York: Viking Press, 1963. Another version of the relevance of the biography to the poetry.

Arthur Carr. "John Keats' Other 'Urn,'" *University of Kansas City Review* XX (Summer, 1954), 237–242. Similarities of outlook in the "Ode on a Grecian Urn" and "The Eve of St. Agnes."

Claude Lee Finney. *"Hyperion, The Eve of St. Agnes, Etc.,"* Chapter six of *The Evolution of Keats' Poetry*, Vol. II. New York: Russell and Russell, 1963. Detailed discussion of Keats's sources and imagery.

Roger Sharrock. "Keats and the Young Lovers," *Review of English Literature*, II (January, 1961), 76–86. Examines Keats as "supremely the adolescent poet."

Dorothy Van Ghent. "Keats' Myth of the Hero," *Keats-Shelley Journal*, III (1954), 7–25.

W. S. Ward. "A Device of Doors in *The Eve of St. Agnes*," *Modern Language Notes*, LXXIII (February, 1958), 90–91. Briefly makes an interesting point on the framing of the poem.

TWENTIETH CENTURY
INTERPRETATIONS

MAYNARD MACK, *Series Editor*
Yale University

NOW AVAILABLE
Collections of Critical Essays
ON

(continued on next page)

(continued from previous page)

MEASURE FOR MEASURE
THE MERCHANT OF VENICE
MOLL FLANDERS
MOLLOY, MALONE DIES, THE UNNAMABLE
MUCH ADO ABOUT NOTHING
THE NIGGER OF THE "NARCISSUS"
OEDIPUS REX
THE OLD MAN AND THE SEA
PAMELA
A PASSAGE TO INDIA
THE PLAYBOY OF THE WESTERN WORLD
POE'S TALES
THE PORTRAIT OF A LADY
A PORTRAIT OF THE ARTIST AS A YOUNG MAN
THE PRAISE OF FOLLY
PRIDE AND PREJUDICE
THE RAINBOW
THE RAPE OF THE LOCK
THE RIME OF THE ANCIENT MARINER
ROBINSON CRUSOE
ROMEO AND JULIET
SAMSON AGONISTES
THE SCARLET LETTER
SIR GAWAIN AND THE GREEN KNIGHT
SONGS OF INNOCENCE AND OF EXPERIENCE
THE SOUND AND THE FURY
THE TEMPEST
TESS OF THE D'URBERVILLES
TOM JONES
TO THE LIGHTHOUSE
THE TURN OF THE SCREW
TWELFTH KNIGHT
UTOPIA
VANITY FAIR
WALDEN
THE WASTE LAND
WOMEN IN LOVE
WUTHERING HEIGHTS